يَٰٓأَيُّهَا ٱلنَّاسُ قَدْ جَآءَتْكُم مَّوْعِظَةٌ
مِّن رَّبِّكُمْ وَشِفَآءٌ لِّمَا فِى ٱلصُّدُورِ وَهُدًى وَرَحْمَةٌ
لِّلْمُؤْمِنِينَ ٥٧

"O mankind, there has to come to you instruction from your Lord and healing for what is in the breasts and guidance and mercy for the believers."

Qur'ān 10:57

MEADOWS *of the* DIVINE

40 Prophetic Traditions on the Virtues & Rulings of the Qur'ān

Alomgir Ali

Foreword by Dr. Haitham al-Haddad

FIGTREE
PUBLICATIONS

British Library Cataloguing in Publishing Data
A catalogue record of this book is available from the British Library.
ISBN: 978-0-9930201-0-0

Title Meadows of the Divine: *40 Prophetic Traditions on the Virtues & Rulings of the Qur'ān*
Author Alomgir Ali

First Edition 20th of Ramaḍān 1435 corresponding to 19th of July, 2014

Cover Design Fig tree Publications
Design & Typesetting Fig tree Publications
Proof reader Aysha Syed

Printed in Turkey by Mega Printing | export@mega.com.tr

FigTree Publications
56 Greenfield Road
London
E1 1EJ
info@figtreepublications.co.uk
www.figtreepublications.co.uk

Fig tree Publications is a project of the Muslim Research & Development Foundation (MRDF)

Charity No. 1119977

After praising and thanking Allāh ﷻ, I must thank those who worked hard to help make the publication of this book a reality. In particular, I would like to thank Sheikh Haitham al-Haddad for checking the text and writing the foreword. I would also like to thank those who helped with the proofreading of the text. I would also like to thank FigTree Publishers for typesetting and designing the book.

Finally, I would like to thank Sheikh 'Ali 'Abd al Tawwāb, a master of the modes of recitation, for being an inspiration behind my love of the Qur'ān. His impeccable manners and humble character helped me to appreciate the greatness of the Qur'ān after seeing how the Qur'ān shaped his character.

Contents

FOREWARD x

INTRODUCTION xii

VIRTUES ON THE QUR'ĀN 1

1. The Virtue of Learning and Teaching the Qur'ān 2

2. The Virtue of Striving to Recite and Memorise the Qur'ān Well 3

3. The People of the Qur'ān are the People of Allāh 4

4. The People of the Qur'ān Deserve to be Envied 5

5. The People of the Qur'ān are More Entitled to Lead People in Prayer 6

6. The Qur'ān Elevates Some and Debases Others 8

7. The Qur'ān Honours the Parents of the People of the Qur'ān 9

8. The Analogy of the Believer Who Recites the Qur'ān and the Believer Who Does Not 10

9. The Vast Amount of Reward for Reciting the Qur'ān 12

10. Holding onto the Qur'ān Prevents Misguidance 13

11. The Qur'ān is an Intercessor 14

12. The Qur'ān Elevates a Person's Level in Paradise 15

13. The Virtue of Listening to the Qur'ān from Others 16

14. The Best Reciter of the Qur'ān 18

15. The Virtue of Reciting and Studying the Qur'ān in the House of Allāh 19

16. The State of the Heart that Knows No Qur'ān 20

17. The Presence of the Angels when the Qur'ān is Recited 21

18. The Virtue of Reciting from the Muṣḥaf 23

19. The Qur'ān Removes Sorrow and Anxiety 24

20. The Qur'ān is a Light for the One Who Recites it 26

21. Allāh Gives to those Preoccupied with the Qur'ān More than He does to those Who Call upon Him 27

22. The Virtue of Reciting the Qur'ān at Night while in Prayer 28

23. The Devil Flees from the Home where Sūrah al Baqarah is Recited 29

24. Contemplating the Words of Allāh 30

25. Honouring the Bearer of the Qur'ān is Veneration of Allāh 32

26. Reciting the Qur'ān by one Who is More Skilled to one Who is Inferior to him, and the Excellence of the People of the Qur'ān 33

27. The Virtue of Being Consistent in the Recitation of the Qur'ān and the Danger of Not Being Consistent in it 34

28. The Virtue of Repeating Verses 35

RULINGS RELATED TO THE QUR'ĀN 37

29. Seeking Refuge in Allāh Before Reciting 38

30. Only the Ritually Pure Should Touch the Qur'ān 40

31. Can the Sexually Impure or Menstruating Women recite the Qur'ān? 42

32. The Importance of Reciting the Qur'ān with a Melodious Voice 43

33. Reciting According to the Way of the Prophet 45

34. The Prostration of Recitation 46

35. Speculative Argumentation over the Qur'ān is Disbelief 48

36. How Often Should One Recite the Qur'ān? 49

37. Reciting the Qur'ān with Meaning and Supplicating During its Recitation 50

38. The Ruling of Reciting the Qur'ān Aloud 52

39. Asking for Money Due to the Recitation of the Qur'ān 53

40. The Obligation of Being Sincere to the Qur'ān 55

REFERENCES 58

Foreword

The Qur'ān is the only divine speech preserved for humanity in its entirety.

إِنَّا نَحْنُ نَزَّلْنَا ٱلذِّكْرَ وَإِنَّا لَهُۥ لَحَـٰفِظُونَ ﴿٩﴾

Allāh ﷻ says, "We have, without doubt, sent down the Qur'ān; and We will assuredly guard it (from corruption)."[1]

It is the most blessed speech that was revealed to the most blessed Prophet in the most blessed place at the most blessed time. Individuals and societies that follow it will therefore be the most blessed ones. As it is divine, Allāh ﷻ honoured it with many unique qualities. It is the only guiding light and humanity cannot traverse a true and straight path except via the light of the Qur'ān.

الٓر ۚ كِتَـٰبٌ أَنزَلْنَـٰهُ إِلَيْكَ لِتُخْرِجَ ٱلنَّاسَ مِنَ ٱلظُّلُمَـٰتِ
إِلَى ٱلنُّورِ بِإِذْنِ رَبِّهِمْ إِلَىٰ صِرَٰطِ ٱلْعَزِيزِ ٱلْحَمِيدِ ﴿١﴾

Allāh ﷻ says, "Alif, Lam, Ra. [This is] a Book which We have revealed to you, [O Muhammad], that you might bring mankind out of darknesses into the light by permission of their Lord - to the path of the Exalted in Might, the Praiseworthy."[2]

Recitation of the Qur'ān is an act of worship.

Ibn Mas'ūd ﷺ reported: The Messenger of Allāh ﷺ said, "Whoever recites a letter from the Book of Allāh ﷻ, he will be credited with a good deed, and a good deed gets a ten-fold reward. I do not say that Alif-Lām-Mīm is one letter, but Alif is a letter, Lām is a letter and Mīm is a letter."[3]

Numerous virtues and qualities of the Qur'ān are listed in this highly beneficial book Sheikh Alomgir Ali has compiled. He followed the practice of many scholars who collected forty statements of the Prophet ﷺ on a specific topic or theme. The prophetic statements in this booklet cover the most important of what the Prophet ﷺ said about the Qur'ān.

MRDF are pleased to have commissioned and published this work and hope it is the first of many publications to enrich our understanding and practice. We ask Allāh ﷻ to make us among the people of the Qur'ān who are His own people and to accept it from the author and publishing team.

Dr. Haitham al Haddad
London, UK
20th of Ramaḍān, 1435
19th of July, 2014

Introduction

'Uthmān ﷺ said, "If your hearts were truly pure, you would not have enough of the Qur'ān. I do not like for one day and night to pass by except that I have to look at the book of Allāh ﷻ." [4]

Feeling estranged from the book of Allāh ﷻ is one of the greatest calamities that can afflict a person, whilst being close to the book of Allāh ﷻ is one of the greatest favours that He ﷻ can bestow upon a person. However, it is important to note that the goal of our relationship with the Qur'ān should not be one based upon the aim to experience spiritual ecstasy and upliftment or based upon the goal to appreciate its eloquence and beauty. Rather it is a book that was sent to guide mankind from darkness into light and to shape our outlook on life:

الٓر ۚ كِتَٰبٌ أَنزَلْنَٰهُ إِلَيْكَ لِتُخْرِجَ ٱلنَّاسَ مِنَ ٱلظُّلُمَٰتِ
إِلَى ٱلنُّورِ بِإِذْنِ رَبِّهِمْ إِلَىٰ صِرَٰطِ ٱلْعَزِيزِ ٱلْحَمِيدِ ﴿١﴾

"Alif, Lām, Rā. [This is] a Book which We have revealed to you, [O Muhammad], that you might bring mankind out of darknesses into the light by permission of their Lord - to the path of the Exalted in Might, the Praiseworthy." [5]

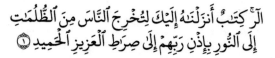

The Qur'ān deserves not to be used as a mere slogan, or a book that is simply referred to in order to find out juristic rulings or scientific facts alone. It should be a book that people turn to for all matters in life, like a man dying of thirst desires water. For many though, they have either yet to feel the urgency of this need or they simply do not appreciate the omnipotence of the book of Allāh ﷻ.

Nevertheless, in recent years there has been a concerted effort in large parts of the Western community to try and restore the ultimate role of the Qur'ān as a complete and comprehensive guide for mankind. Many people are taking a keener interest in the study of the *tafsīr* of the Qur'ān after having tasted the sweetness of understanding the deeper meanings of many chapters of the Qur'ān they had always taken for granted. Such a restoration of consciousness is without doubt welcomed and greeted, and should be encouraged further.

It is with this in mind that I decided to contribute towards the kindling of this spark of light by gathering a collection of prophetic traditions that touch upon various aspects of the virtues of the Qur'ān as well as its rulings. This is all in hope that people will awaken from the slumber that they are in with regards to the book of Allāh ﷻ, and that they appreciate their need for the book of Allāh ﷻ and its greatness.

Methodology of selection of aḥādīth and commentary

1. In keeping with the tradition of many scholars from the past, 40 ḥadīth were chosen in order to make this work accessible to people from all backgrounds. Many classical

works already exist but are quite exhaustive in nature. This particular text was aimed for everyone to benefit from and not just scholars and students of knowledge.

2. I have tried to make the selection of ḥadīth as vast as possible in terms of variety of topics and tried not to mention any ḥadīth which may have been alluded to elsewhere in the book.

3. Although there is a scholarly opinion that states it is permissible to quote weak *aḥādīth* pertaining to virtues under certain conditions, I strove to mention those that have been declared authentic by ḥadīth masters from old and present. This made the task more difficult, especially considering point [2], and so a few of the selected *aḥādīth* remain disputed in terms of authenticity of transmission.[6] Nevertheless, the meanings that they convey are, by the will of Allāh ﷻ, still valid.

4. Most of the commentary is based upon classical explanations of books of ḥadīth, as well as later commentaries such as Ibn Ḥajar's رحمه الله *Fatḥ al Bāri*, al Nawawi's رحمه الله *Sharḥ Ṣaḥiḥ Muslim*, al Khaṭṭābi's رحمه الله *Ma'ālim al Sunan*, Ibn al Baṭṭāl's رحمه الله commentary of *Ṣaḥīḥ al Bukhāri*, Al Munāwi's رحمه الله *Fayḍ al Qadīr* and Mulla Ali Qāri's رحمه الله *Mirqāh al Mafātīḥ*. I avoided mention of detailed commentary and linguistic nuances as I wanted to make this book accessible to as many people as possible. I have occasionally added personal insights and points of reflection.

5. I have attempted to give practical advice where possible as to how these traditions can help develop our relationship with the Qur'ān. These points should be carefully considered since we should not aim to simply

be awestruck by these traditions, rather we should strive to make the teachings and wisdoms that these traditions impart leave an imprint on our lives.

6. I have also included a number of traditions that relate to rulings (*aḥkām*) of the Qur'ān. If we seek to live a life with the Qur'ān, we ought to know the correct etiquette in how to deal with the Qur'ān, since venerating it is a sign of our veneration of Allāh ﷻ. In areas where there are differences of opinion, I have tried to briefly mention the various views regarding those issues with emphasis given to those views that were upheld by the majority of classical jurists.

May Allāh ﷻ benefit the *ummah* through this work, turn our hearts towards His book and make us from the people of the Qur'ān. *Āmīn.*

Alomgir Ali
Muslim Research & Development Foundation
London, UK
20th of Ramaḍān, 1435
19th of July, 2014

Virtues
of the Qur'ān
aḥādīth 1-28

Ḥadīth no.1

The Virtue of Learning and Teaching the Qur'ān

عَنْ عُثْمَانَ رَضِيَ اللهُ عَنْهُ، عَنِ النَّبِيِّ صَلَّى اللهُ عَلَيْهِ وَسَلَّمَ قَالَ :

خَيْرُكُمْ مَنْ تَعَلَّمَ القُرْآنَ وَعَلَّمَهُ.

رَوَاهُ البُخَارِي

'Uthmān ﷺ reported that the Prophet ﷺ said, "The best of you are those who learn the Qur'ān and teach it."[7]

✿ 'The best of you...' is a phrase the Prophet ﷺ used on a number of occasions to encourage people to adopt certain characteristics, and to establish the virtue of those who adopt such traits.

✿ The nobility of a discipline is dependent upon the topic of that discipline, and the topic of the Qur'ān is the very speech of Allāh ﷻ. Hence, the person who learns and teaches it in a comprehensive way deserves to be the best of mankind.

✿ Such people are the best because there is no better way to benefit oneself and others than by the Qur'ān. Thus, the bearers of the Qur'ān have been likened to the noble Angels who pass on revelation to mankind, as they also pass on revelation to mankind.

✿ The Prophet ﷺ combined the mention of two types of benefits: one that is *qāṣir* (limited to oneself) and another that is *muta'addin* (benefitting others). The believer should aspire to be of those who not only benefit themselves, but also benefit others. Allāh ﷻ says, *"And who is better in speech than one who invites to Allāh and does righteousness and says, 'Indeed, I am of the Muslims.'"[8]* In this verse both types of benefits are also mentioned.

✿ It is implied therefore that the worst type of people are those who do not learn the Qur'ān and also prevent others from learning it.[9] Allāh ﷻ says, *"Indeed, those who disbelieve and avert [people] from the way of Allāh have certainly gone far astray."*[10]

Ḥadīth no.2

The Virtue of Striving to Recite and Memorise the Qur'ān Well

عَنْ عَائِشَةَ رَضِيَ اللَّهُ عَنْهَا، قَالَتْ: قَالَ رَسُولُ اللَّهِ صَلَّى اللَّهُ عَلَيْهِ وَسَلَّمَ:

الْمَاهِرُ بِالْقُرْآنِ مَعَ السَّفَرَةِ الْكِرَامِ الْبَرَرَةِ، وَالَّذِي يَقْرَأُ الْقُرْآنَ وَيَتَتَعْتَعُ فِيهِ، وَهُوَ عَلَيْهِ شَاقٌّ، لَهُ أَجْرَانِ.

رَوَاهُ مُسْلِم

A'ishah رضي الله عنها reported that the Prophet ﷺ said, "The proficient (māhir) reciter of the Qur'ān will be with the noble righteous scribes, and the one who recites it and stumbles in its recitation while it is difficult for him will have two rewards."[11]

۞ Al Nawawi رحمه الله described the *māhir* as being "proficient, someone who has memorised the Qur'ān in its entirety (*kāmil al hifẓ*), such that he does not hesitate in its recitation nor is it difficult for him due to the precision of his memorisation."[12]

۞ *Safarah* (scribes [pl. of *sāfir* or *safīr*]). Lexically, safr means to clarify or make clear. If it is the plural of *sāfir* then it refers to a writer (*kātib*) as they make matters clear with their writing. If, on the other hand, it is the plural of *safīr*, then it refers to someone who rectifies the affairs between two people. Both meanings are applicable to the Noble Angels of Allāh ﷻ since they convey revelation to creation and they reform people's lives by it.

✪ The reason why the proficient reciter who is a *hāfiẓ* is likened to such Angels is due to the similarity between them. They both help propagate and preserve the words of Allāh ﷻ and will therefore be ranked together in the Afterlife.

✪ The last part of the ḥadīth should not be understood to mean that the one who struggles with the recitation of the Qur'ān will have *double* the reward of the proficient reciter. On the contrary, the proficient reciter will receive far more reward since it takes much time and effort to become a proficient reciter and memoriser of the Qur'ān. The one who struggles receives *two* rewards; one for the recitation and another for experiencing the hardship connected to it.

Ḥadīth no.3

The People of the Qur'ān are the People of Allāh ﷻ

عَنْ أَنَسٍ رَضِيَ اللّٰهُ عَنْهُ قَالَ: قَالَ رَسُولُ اللّٰهِ صَلَّى اللّٰهُ عَلَيْهِ وَسَلَّمَ:

إِنَّ لِلَّهِ أَهْلِينَ مِنَ النَّاسِ قَالَ: قِيلَ: مَنْ هُمْ يَا رَسُولَ اللّٰهِ؟ قَالَ: أَهْلُ الْقُرْآنِ هُمْ أَهْلُ اللّٰهِ، وَخَاصَّتُهُ.

رَوَاهُ الإِمَامُ أَحْمَد فِي المُسْنَدِ

Anas ؓ reported that the Prophet ﷺ said, "To Allāh ﷻ belongs a special group of people." It was said, "Who are they, O Messenger of Allāh?" He ﷺ replied, "They are the people of the Qur'ān; the people of Allāh ﷻ, and his select group of people."[13]

✪ Belonging to Allāh ﷻ means to be specially honoured by Allāh ﷻ.

✪ The people of Qur'ān are those who read it, understand its meanings, reflect upon its verses and act in accordance with its teachings.

The ḥadīth teaches us to honour the people of the Qur'ān and to follow them in their positive traits.

Ḥadīth no.4

The People of the Qur'ān Deserve to be Envied

عَنْ أَبِي هُرَيْرَةَ رَضِيَ اللَّهُ عَنْهُ أَنَّ رَسُولَ اللَّهِ صَلَّى اللهُ عَلَيْهِ وَسَلَّمَ قَالَ:

لاَ حَسَدَ إِلَّا فِي اثْنَتَيْنِ: رَجُلٌ عَلَّمَهُ اللَّهُ القُرْآنَ، فَهُوَ يَتْلُوهُ آنَاءَ اللَّيْلِ، وَآنَاءَ النَّهَارِ، فَسَمِعَهُ جَارٌ لَهُ، فَقَالَ: لَيْتَنِي أُوتِيتُ مِثْلَ مَا أُوتِيَ فُلاَنٌ، فَعَمِلْتُ مِثْلَ مَا يَعْمَلُ، وَرَجُلٌ آتَاهُ اللَّهُ مَالًا فَهُوَ يُهْلِكُهُ فِي الحَقِّ، فَقَالَ رَجُلٌ: لَيْتَنِي أُوتِيتُ مِثْلَ مَا أُوتِيَ فُلاَنٌ، فَعَمِلْتُ مِثْلَ مَا يَعْمَلُ.

رواه البُخاري

Abū Hurayrah reported that the Prophet said, "No one should envy another person with exception to two people: a man whom Allāh taught the Qur'ān and so he recites it day and night. His neighbour then hears him and says, 'If only I was given what he was given and did what he does.' And a man whom Allāh had given wealth which he spends for noble causes and so a person would say, 'If only I was given what he was given and did what he does."[14]

The '*envy*' that is mentioned in this ḥadīth is in reference to a permissible form of 'envy' known as *ghibṭah*, i.e. wishing for what someone else has without wishing for that blessing to be taken away from that person. *Ghibṭah* is not blameworthy in essence unlike *ḥasad*, which is to wish to have what someone else has whilst wishing for that blessing to be taken away from that person.

۞ Wishing to have the same righteous traits of others is praiseworthy, especially when those righteous traits are very lofty like being from the people of the Qur'ān.

۞ The Prophet ﷺ combined the mention of two types of acts of worship; those that pertain to one's own self; and those that involve wealth. This shows us the importance of diversity in the acts of worship.

۞ The ḥadīth also teaches us the areas of life in which we should aspire and desire to be like others.

۞ The use of the word '*given*' in the ḥadīth reinforces the notion that it is by the *tawfīq* (divine assistance) of Allāh ﷻ that a person becomes from amongst the people of the Qur'ān. Therefore, a person should strive to ask Allāh ﷻ to make him from the people of the Qur'ān as well as undertake the necessary actions that will grant him this *tawfīq* from Allāh ﷻ.

Ḥadīth no.5

The People of the Qur'ān are More Entitled to Lead People in Prayer

عَنْ أَبِي مَسْعُودٍ الْأَنْصَارِيِّ رَضِيَ اللَّهُ عَنْهُ، قَالَ: قَالَ رَسُولُ اللهِ صَلَّى اللهُ عَلَيْهِ وَسَلَّمَ:

يَؤُمُّ الْقَوْمَ أَقْرَؤُهُمْ لِكِتَابِ اللهِ، فَإِنْ كَانُوا فِي الْقِرَاءَةِ سَوَاءً، فَأَعْلَمُهُمْ بِالسُّنَّةِ، فَإِنْ كَانُوا فِي السُّنَّةِ سَوَاءً، فَأَقْدَمُهُمْ هِجْرَةً، فَإِنْ كَانُوا فِي الْهِجْرَةِ سَوَاءً، فَأَقْدَمُهُمْ سِلْمًا، وَلَا يَؤُمَّنَّ الرَّجُلَ الرَّجُلَ فِي سُلْطَانِهِ، وَلَا يَقْعُدْ فِي بَيْتِهِ عَلَى تَكْرِمَتِهِ إِلَّا بِإِذْنِهِ.

قَالَ الْأَشَجُّ فِي رِوَايَتِهِ مَكَانَ سِلْمًا: سِنًّا. رَوَاهُ مُسْلِم

Abū Mas'ūd al-Anṣāri reported Allāh's Messenger ﷺ as saying, "The one who is most versed in Allāh's Book should act as Imām for the people, but if they are equally versed in reciting it, then the one who has most knowledge regarding Sunnah. If they are equal regarding the Sunnah, then the earliest one to emigrate; if they emigrated at the same time, then the earliest one to embrace Islam. No man must lead another in prayer where [the latter] has authority, or sit in his place of honour in his house, without his permission. Ashajj ⁕ used the word 'age' in place of 'Islam' in his narration."[15]

❂ Being more versed in the Qur'ān entitles a person to be the Imām in prayer.

❂ The scholars differ as to what the term *aqra'* means. Some scholars such as the *shāfi'is* say it refers to the most learned, whereas others such as the *ḥanābilah* say it refers to the more proficient reciter who has memorised the most.

❂ Ibn Qudāmah ⁕ said, "If one is a more skilled reciter (*ajwad*) whilst another person has memorised more Qur'ān, the more skilled reciter is more entitled to lead the people in prayer."[16]

❂ If both are equally as proficient in the quality of their recitation, then the one who has memorised the most is more entitled to lead the people in prayer.

Ḥadīth no.6

The Qur'ān Elevates Some and Debases Others

عن عَامِرُ بْنُ وَاثِلَةَ رَضِيَ اللَّهُ عَنْهُ:

أَنَّ نَافِعَ بْنَ عَبْدِ الْحَارِثِ لَقِيَ عُمَرَ بْنَ الْخَطَّابِ بِعُسْفَانَ، وَكَانَ عُمَرُ اسْتَعْمَلَهُ عَلَى أَهْلِ مَكَّةَ، فَسَلَّمَ عَلَى عُمَرَ، فَقَالَ لَهُ عُمَرُ: مَنِ اسْتَخْلَفْتَ عَلَى أَهْلِ الْوَادِي؟ فَقَالَ نَافِعٌ: اسْتَخْلَفْتُ عَلَيْهِمْ ابْنَ أَبْزَى. فَقَالَ عُمَرُ: وَمَنْ ابْنُ أَبْزَى؟ فَقَالَ: مَوْلًى مِنْ مَوَالِينَا. فَقَالَ عُمَرُ: فَاسْتَخْلَفْتَ عَلَيْهِمْ مَوْلًى؟ فَقَالَ: يَا أَمِيرَ الْمُؤْمِنِينَ إِنَّهُ قَارِئٌ لِكِتَابِ اللَّهِ، عَالِمٌ بِالْفَرَائِضِ. فَقَالَ عُمَرُ: أَمَا إِنَّ رَسُولَ اللَّهِ صَلَّى اللَّهُ عَلَيْهِ وَسَلَّمَ قَدْ قَالَ: إِنَّ اللَّهَ يَرْفَعُ بِهَذَا الْكِتَابِ أَقْوَامًا، وَيَضَعُ بِهِ آخَرِينَ.

رَوَاهُ مُسْلم

'Amir bin Wāthilah reported that Nāfi' bin 'Abd al-Ḥārith met 'Umar at 'Usfān and 'Umar had employed him as a deputy over the people in Mecca. He ['Umar] said to him [Nāfi'], "Whom have you appointed as a deputy over the people of the valley?" He said, "Ibn Abzā." He said, "Who is Ibn Abzā?" He said, "He is one of our freed slaves." He ['Umar] said, "So you have appointed a freed slave over them?" He said, "He is well versed in the Book of Allah and he is well versed in the laws of inheritance." 'Umar said, "If that is the case, then indeed the Prophet ﷺ said, 'Allāh exalts some people by this book and debases others by it.'"[17]

✿ The Qur'ān elevates those that memorise and act upon it in this life by giving them an honourable and respectful life.

- As for those who shun it and turn away from its teachings, they will have a miserable and lowly life.
- Al Ṭībī said, "Whoever reads the Qur'ān [and] acts in accordance to it *sincerely*, Allāh will elevate his ranks, but whoever reads it with ostentation and does not act according to it will be debased by Allāh."
- This ḥadīth teaches us that the benefits of the Qur'ān are not restricted to the Afterlife; rather its positive effects can be experienced and witnessed in this life as well.

Ḥadīth no.7

The Qur'ān Honours the Parents of the People of the Qur'ān

عَنْ بُرَيْدَةَ رَضِيَ اللهُ عَنْهُ قَالَ قَالَ رَسُولُ اللهِ صَلَّى اللهُ عَلَيْهِ وَسَلَّمَ:

مَنْ قَرَأَ الْقُرْآنَ وَتَعَلَّمَ وَعَمِلَ بِهِ أُلْبِسَ وَالِدَاهُ يَوْمَ الْقِيَامَةِ تَاجاً مِنْ نُورٍ ضَوْؤُهُ مِثْلُ ضَوْءِ الشَّمْسِ وَيُكْسَى وَالِدَاهُ حُلَّتَيْنِ لا يَقُومُ لَهُمَا الدُّنْيَا فَيَقُولانِ بِمَ كُسِينَا هَذا؟ فَيُقَالُ بِأَخْذِ وَلَدِكُمَا القُرْآنَ.

رَوَاهُ الحَاكِم فِي المُسْتَدْرَك

Buraydah reported that the Prophet said, "Whoever reads the Qur'ān, learns from it and acts upon it will have his parents crowned with a crown of light; its light will be like the light of the sun. His parents will also be gowned with two garments that are more valuable than the dunyā and they will say, 'Why were we clothed with this?' And it will be said, 'Due to your son taking the Qur'ān.'"[18]

✪ This is in reference to the one who studied, memorised and acted upon the Qur'ān.

✪ If this is the honour given to the parents of the people of the Qur'ān, then imagine what would be the reward of the people of the Qur'ān themselves!

✪ This ḥadīth teaches us how much Allāh ﷻ loves the people of the Qur'ān; to the extent that He will also honour those who are close to the people of the Qur'ān.

Ḥadīth no.8

The Analogy of the Believer Who Recites the Qur'ān and the Believer Who Does Not

عَنْ أَبِي مُوسَى الأَشْعَرِيِّ رَضِيَ اللهُ عَنْهُ، قَالَ: قَالَ رَسُولُ اللهِ صَلَّى اللهُ عَلَيْهِ وَسَلَّمَ:

مَثَلُ المُؤْمِنِ الَّذِي يَقْرَأُ القُرْآنَ كَمَثَلِ الأُتْرُجَّةِ، رِيحُهَا طَيِّبٌ وَطَعْمُهَا طَيِّبٌ، وَمَثَلُ المُؤْمِنِ الَّذِي لاَ يَقْرَأُ القُرْآنَ كَمَثَلِ التَّمَرَةِ، لاَ رِيحَ لَهَا وَطَعْمُهَا حُلْوٌ، وَمَثَلُ المُنَافِقِ الَّذِي يَقْرَأُ القُرْآنَ مَثَلُ الرَّيْحَانَةِ، رِيحُهَا طَيِّبٌ وَطَعْمُهَا مُرٌّ، وَمَثَلُ المُنَافِقِ الَّذِي لاَ يَقْرَأُ القُرْآنَ كَمَثَلِ الحَنْظَلَةِ، لَيْسَ لَهَا رِيحٌ وَطَعْمُهَا مُرٌّ.

رَوَاهُ البُخَارِي

Abū Mūsā al-Ashʿari ❀ *reported that Allāh's Messenger* ❀ *said, "A believer who recites the Qur'ān regularly is like a citron whose fragrance is sweet and whose taste is good; a believer who does not recite the Qur'ān regularly is like a date which has no fragrance but has a sweet taste; and the hypocrite who recites the Qur'ān regularly is like basil whose fragrance is sweet but whose taste is bitter; and a hypocrite who does not recite the Qur'ān regularly is like the colocynth, which has no fragrance and has a bitter taste."[19]*

۞ The citron was singled out due to its numerous benefits and features. Its taste, fragrance and appearance were very pleasing to the Arabs, and its skin had medicinal properties. It was also pressed for beneficial oils.

۞ The Prophet ﷺ mentioned two features of the citron; its taste and fragrance. The taste represents the faith of the believer while the fragrance represents the recitation of the believer. As faith is a more constant feature of the believer compared to their recitation, taste was used, which is the internal feature of the citron. On the other hand, recitation is not as consistent as faith and so fragrance was used to represent it.

۞ Like pleasant fragrances, recitation affects others around those who recite the Qur'ān. They find peace upon hearing its recitation and earn reward for listening to it. Likewise, the character of the people of the Qur'ān influences others due to its resonance with the teachings of the Qur'ān.

۞ The believer who does not regularly recite the Qur'ān still has faith, and so is likened to a date that has a pleasant taste. However, it has no fragrance and so is not as influential as the one who regularly recites and learns the Qur'ān.

۞ The difference between the pip of the citron and the date also reflects the heart of the one who recites the Qur'ān and the one who does not. The pip of the citron is white and smooth whereas the pip of the date is dark and rough. The Qur'ān cleanses and softens the heart and so without it our hearts grow dark and become tarnished.

۞ Ibn Ḥajar رحمه الله mentioned that it was said that jinns flee from homes that have citron in them just as the devils flee from homes where the Qur'ān is recited.

Ḥadīth no.9

The Vast Amount of Reward for Reciting the Qur'ān

عن عَبْدَ اللهِ بْنَ مَسْعُودٍ رَضِيَ اللَّهُ عَنْهُ، يَقُولُ: قَالَ رَسُولُ اللهِ صَلَّى اللَّهُ عَلَيْهِ وَسَلَّمَ:

مَنْ قَرَأَ حَرْفًا مِنْ كِتَابِ اللهِ فَلَهُ بِهِ حَسَنَةٌ، وَالحَسَنَةُ بِعَشْرِ أَمْثَالِهَا، لاَ أَقُولُ الم حَرْفٌ، وَلكِنْ أَلِفٌ حَرْفٌ وَلاَمٌ حَرْفٌ وَمِيمٌ حَرْفٌ.

رَواهُ التِّرمِذِي

'Abdullāh Ibn Mas'ūd ﷺ reported that the Messenger of Allāh ﷺ said, "Whoever recites a letter from the Book of Allāh ﷻ will be rewarded with a good deed, and a good deed gets a ten-fold reward. I do not say that Alif-Lām-Mīm is one letter, but Alif is a letter, Lām is a letter and Mīm is a letter."[20]

- Due to the blessings of the Qur'ān, a person is rewarded for its mere recitation even without understanding what one reads. However, without a shadow of a doubt, reciting whilst understanding its meaning is more virtuous.
- Those who struggle to understand the Qur'ān in Arabic should not find the mere recitation of the Qur'ān as pointless, as the potential reward for its recitation is overwhelming.
- One can recite the Qur'ān for a number of different motives in addition to seeking the pleasure of Allāh ﷻ. It is important that we are aware of this in order to make our relationship with the Qur'ān dynamic and as beneficial as possible. One can recite the Qur'ān for:
    - Reward and blessings
    - Contemplation and reflection (in order to act upon it)
    - Memorisation
    - Revision
    - Seeking cures for spiritual and physical ailments etc.

Ḥadīth no.10

Holding onto the Qur'ān Prevents Misguidance

عَنْ أَبِي شُرَيْحٍ الْخُزَاعِيِّ رَضِيَ اللَّهُ عَنْهُ، قَالَ:

خَرَجَ عَلَيْنَا رَسُولُ اللَّهِ صَلَّى اللَّهُ عَلَيْهِ وَسَلَّمَ، فَقَالَ: أَبْشِرُوا وَأَبْشِرُوا، أَلَيْسَ تَشْهَدُونَ أَنْ لَا إِلَهَ إِلَّا اللَّهُ، وَأَنِّي رَسُولُ اللَّهِ؟ قَالُوا: نَعَمْ، قَالَ: فَإِنَّ هَذَا الْقُرْآنَ سَبَبٌ طَرَفُهُ بِيَدِ اللَّهِ، وَطَرَفُهُ بِأَيْدِيكُمْ، فَتَمَسَّكُوا بِهِ، فَإِنَّكُمْ لَنْ تَضِلُّوا، وَلَنْ تَهْلِكُوا بَعْدَهُ أَبَدًا.

رَوَاهُ ابنُ حِبَّان في صَحِيحِهِ

Abū Shurayḥ al Khuzāʿi ﵁ said, "The Prophet ﷺ one day came out to us and said, 'Have glad tidings! Have glad tidings! Do you not bear witness that none has the right to be worshipped except Allāh ﷻ and that I am the Messenger of Allāh?' They said, 'Yes.' He ﷺ then said, 'Then indeed this Qur'ān is a rope. One end is in the Hand of Allāh ﷻ and the other end is in your hands, so adhere to it for you will not be misguided or destroyed after that.'"[21]

✿ The word used for rope here, '*sabab*', was traditionally used to refer to ropes that were hung from above, as in from a ceiling or a roof. Therefore, it denotes a sense of escape from danger or harm. The Qur'ān, likewise, saves people from destruction and harm in this life and the Afterlife on condition that they adhere to its teachings.

✿ Al Ṭībī ﵀ said, "Whoever abandons acting upon a verse or one word from the Qur'ān which is obligatory to act upon, or abandons reciting it out of pride, disbelieves. However, whoever leaves it out of inability, laziness or weakness, yet still venerates the Qur'ān, is not sinful due to not reciting it. However, such a person is *maḥrūm* (deprived from good)."[22]

- The ḥadīth teaches us to appreciate the Qur'ān and to rejoice for Allāh ﷻ has given us protection and the key to our success.

Ḥadīth no.11

The Qur'ān is an Intercessor

عَنْ عَبْدِ اللهِ بْنِ مَسْعُودٍ رَضِيَ اللَّهُ عَنْهُ قَالَ: قَالَ رَسُولُ اللهِ صَلَّى اللهُ عَلَيْهِ وَسَلَّمَ:

الْقُرْآنُ شَافِعٌ مُشَفَّعٌ وَمَاحِلٌ مُصَدَّقٌ مَنْ جَعَلَهُ أَمَامَهُ قَادَهُ إِلَى الْجَنَّةِ وَمَنْ جَعَلَهُ خَلْفَ ظَهْرِهِ سَاقَهُ إِلَى النَّارِ.

رَوَاهُ الطَّبَرَانِي فِي الْمُعْجَمِ الْكَبِيرِ

'Abdullāh bin Mas'ūd ؓ reported that The Prophet ﷺ said, "The Qur'ān will be an accepted intercessor and a believed adversary. Whoever places it in front of him, it will lead him to Paradise, and whoever places it behind him, it will drive him to the Fire."[23]

- This will be for the people of the Qur'ān and those that dedicated themselves to it.
- It will be an intercessor by appearing in the form of an entity that will intercede for the people of the Qur'ān.
- Placing the Qur'ān in front of you means to allow the Qur'ān to guide you. We should not approach the Qur'ān with preconceived notions of right and wrong, but should rather allow the Qur'ān to determine that for us. Unfortunately, many people subconsciously approach the Qur'ān having already determined for themselves what guidance is and therefore look to the Qur'ān for those passages that conform to their understanding and shun that which disagrees with it.
- A person who shuns the Qur'ān will fall into misguidance as it is only through the Qur'ān that we can be guided.

Ḥadīth no.12

The Qur'ān Elevates a Person's Level in Paradise

عَنْ عَبْدِ اللَّهِ بْنِ عَمْرٍو رَضِيَ اللَّهُ عَنْهُ، قَالَ: قَالَ رَسُولُ اللَّهِ صَلَّى اللهُ عَلَيْهِ وَسَلَّمَ:

يُقَالُ لِصَاحِبِ الْقُرْآنِ: اقْرَأْ، وَارْتَقِ، وَرَتِّلْ كَمَا كُنْتَ تُرَتِّلُ فِي الدُّنْيَا، فَإِنَّ مَنْزِلَكَ عِنْدَ آخِرِ آيَةٍ تَقْرَؤُهَا.

رَوَاهُ التِّرْمِذِي

'Abdullāh bin 'Amr ﷺ said that the Messenger ﷺ said, "It shall be said to the companion of the Qur'ān: 'Recite, and rise up, recite with tartīl (in a well-paced manner) as you would recite in the world. For indeed, your rank shall be determined by the last āyah you recite.'"[24]

- The '*Ṣāḥib al Qur'ān*' (companion of the Qur'ān) is the one who frequently engages in its recitation and acts upon it. Ibn al Qayyim رحمه الله said, "The companion of the Qur'ān is the one who is knowledgeable of it and acts in accordance with it even though he may not have memorised it. As for the one who memorised it but does not understand it, nor does he act upon it, then he is not from its people, even if he recites it with perfection."[25] This ḥadīth, however, is in specific reference to the *ḥāfiẓ* who acted upon what they had memorised.
- This will be said to a person when they enter into Paradise.
- A person's level in Paradise will be determined by how much Qur'ān they memorised. The more they recite, the more they will rise in Paradise.
- *Tartīl* means to recite in an unhurried and measured manner, by clearly pronouncing each letter correctly from its correct articulation point, thus making one's recitation more understandable. If one recites too quickly, it may be difficult to understand what is being recited.

✪ Al Ṭībī رحمه الله said, "This recitation will be like the *tasbīḥ* of the Angels; it will not distract them from enjoying themselves, in fact it will be the greatest enjoyment for them."[26]

✪ The levels in Paradise are in accordance to the number of *āyāt* in the Qur'ān. Therefore, if a person memorises the entire Qur'ān and acts according to its teachings, they will be amongst those who occupy the highest stations in Paradise.

Ḥadīth no.13

The Virtue of Listening to the Qur'ān from Others

عَنْ عَبْدِ اللَّهِ بنِ مَسْعُودٍ رَضِيَ اللَّهُ عَنْهُ قَالَ: قَالَ لِي النَّبِيُّ صَلَّى اللهُ عَلَيْهِ وَسَلَّمَ:

اقْرَأْ عَلَيَّ قُلْتُ: آقْرَأُ عَلَيْكَ وَعَلَيْكَ أُنْزِلَ؟ قَالَ: فَإِنِّي أُحِبُّ أَنْ أَسْمَعَهُ مِنْ غَيْرِي فَقَرَأْتُ عَلَيْهِ سُورَةَ النِّسَاءِ، حَتَّى بَلَغْتُ: فَكَيْفَ إِذَا جِئْنَا مِن كُلِّ أُمَّةٍ بِشَهِيدٍ وَجِئْنَا بِكَ عَلَىٰ هَٰٓؤُلَآءِ شَهِيدًا [النساء: ٤١] قَالَ: أَمْسِكْ فَإِذَا عَيْنَاهُ تَذْرِفَانِ.

رواه البخاري

'Abdullāh bin Mas'ūd ﷺ said, "The Prophet ﷺ said to me, 'Recite to me.' I said, 'Shall I recite it to you even though it has been revealed to you?' He said, 'I like to hear [the Qur'ān] from others.' So I recited Sūrah an-Nisā' until I reached: 'How [will it be] then when We bring from each nation a witness, and We bring you [O Muḥammad] as a witness against these people?' (4:41) Then he said, 'Stop!' And behold, his eyes were overflowing with tears."[27]

✪ Listening to the Qur'ān from others helps one to reflect more upon its meanings rather than reciting it oneself. This is because the reciter needs to concentrate on reciting the Qur'ān correctly, which could reduce their ability to contemplate.

✪ Our relationship with the Qur'ān should not be limited to reciting it ourselves. We should also make the effort to listen to it from others, whether it be in person or through other means such as recordings. However, listening to someone in person is more conducive for reflection and contemplation.

✪ It is recommended to weep upon reciting and listening to the Qur'ān. In a ḥadīth it is stated that "Indeed this Qur'ān was sent down with sadness, so when you recite it, weep, and if you cannot weep, then force yourself to weep..."[28] The companions and the early generations were known for their crying upon hearing and reciting the Qur'ān. Hence, al Nawawi ﷺ said, "Crying when reciting the Qur'ān is the characteristic of those who knew Allāh ﷻ and is the distinguishing mark of the righteous."[29]

✪ Imām al Ghazāli ﷺ said, "Weeping is recommended while reciting the Qur'ān or witnessing its recitation [...] The way to achieve this is by bringing sadness to the mind by pondering the threats and warnings, the covenants and agreements that it contains, and then contemplating one's shortcomings with regard to them. If this does not bring to mind sadness and weeping, as it does with the elite worshippers, then one should weep from the lack of it, since it is among the greatest of calamities."[30]

✪ The Prophet ﷺ either cried upon hearing this verse out of mercy for his *ummah* as he will be a witness for them as well as a witness against them, or he cried over the enormity of the scene that the verse depicts. Some scholars also suggest that he may have cried out of happiness for his *ummah* because his testimony would be accepted, *ṣallalāhu 'alayhi wa sallam*.[31]

✪ When 'Umar ﷺ used to see Abū Mūsā al Ash'ari ﷺ, who was well known for his beautiful recitation of the Qur'ān, he used to say, "Remind us of our Lord, O Abū Mūsa!" and so he would begin to recite.

Ḥadīth no.14

The Best Reciter of the Qur'ān

عَنْ جَابِرٍ رَضِيَ اللَّهُ عَنْهُ، قَالَ: قَالَ رَسُولُ اللَّهِ صَلَّى اللَّهُ عَلَيْهِ وَسَلَّمَ:

إِنَّ مِنْ أَحْسَنِ النَّاسِ صَوْتًا بِالْقُرْآنِ، الَّذِي إِذَا سَمِعْتُمُوهُ يَقْرَأُ، حَسِبْتُمُوهُ يَخْشَى اللَّهَ.

رَوَاهُ ابن ماجه

Jābir said that the Prophet said, "The one who has the best recitation of the Qur'ān is the one who when you hear him you think that he has awe of Allāh."[32]

- If listening to the Qur'ān is virtuous, it is important to know what criteria a person should have for choosing to listen to a particular reciter.
- Pleasant voices are always enjoyable to listen to, but we have to be careful not to make the pleasantness of the voice the sole criteria for the choice of who we listen to. Beautiful recitation of the Qur'ān is like a key that opens up the treasures of the Qur'ān. Therefore, do not use the recitation to marvel at the key but use it as a means of marveling at the treasures that lie beyond the door. As such, beautiful recitation is a means to an end and not the end itself.
- A person who recites with *khashyah* (awe) understands what they are reciting and is clearly moved by it. This person therefore alters their tone based upon the meaning of what they recite.

Ḥadīth no.15

The Virtue of Reciting and Studying the Qur'ān in the House of Allāh ﷻ

عَنْ أَبِي هُرَيْرَةَ رَضِيَ اللهُ عَنْهُ، عَنِ النَّبِيِّ صَلَّى اللهُ عَلَيْهِ وَسَلَّمَ قَالَ:

مَا اجْتَمَعَ قَوْمٌ فِي بَيْتٍ مِنْ بُيُوتِ اللَّهِ تَعَالَى، يَتْلُونَ كِتَابَ اللهِ وَيَتَدَارَسُونَهُ بَيْنَهُمْ، إِلَّا نَزَلَتْ عَلَيْهِمُ السَّكِينَةُ، وَغَشِيَتْهُمُ الرَّحْمَةُ، وَحَفَّتْهُمُ الْمَلَائِكَةُ، وَذَكَرَهُمُ اللهُ فِيمَنْ عِنْدَهُ.

رَوَاهُ أَبُو دَاوُد

Abū Hurairah ؓ reported the Prophet ﷺ as saying, "No people gather together in a house of the houses of Allāh [i.e. a mosque], reciting the Book of Allāh and learning it together among themselves, except that tranquility (sakīnah) descends upon them, [divine] mercy covers them [from above] and the Angels surround them, and Allāh ﷻ makes mention of them among those who are with Him."[33]

- Some scholars are of the view that this also applies to other virtuous places like madrasahs.[34]
- Reciting the Qur'ān to one another in a collective manner is a desirable way of learning and revising the Qur'ān. It is also a way of openly manifesting the speech of Allāh ﷻ.
- The Angels of mercy surround such gatherings.
- Allāh's ﷻ mention of them refers to Allāh ﷻ praising them before His Angels.

Ḥadīth no.16

The State of the Heart that Knows No Qur'ān

عَنِ ابْنِ عَبَّاسٍ رَضِيَ اللَّهُ عَنْهُ، قَالَ: قَالَ رَسُولُ اللهِ صَلَّى اللهُ عَلَيْهِ وَسَلَّمَ:

إِنَّ الَّذِي لَيْسَ فِي جَوْفِهِ شَيْءٌ مِنَ القُرْآنِ، كَالْبَيْتِ الخَرِبِ.

رَوَاهُ التِّرمِذِي

Ibn 'Abbās ﵁ narrated that the Messenger of Allāh ﷺ said, "Indeed, the one who does not have anything of the Qur'ān inside of him [i.e. his heart] is like an uninhabited, derelict house."[35]

✿ Mullā 'Alī al Qāri ﵀ said, "That is because the prosperity of the heart is through faith, recitation of the Qur'ān, adorning the inner state by adopting correct tenants of creed, and reflecting over the blessings of Allāh ﷻ."[36]

✿ The Qur'ān therefore rectifies one's inner state if it is approached in the correct manner. One should recite and learn the Qur'ān with this aim in mind. Allāh ﷻ also calls the Qur'ān '*rūḥ*' (spirit/soul),[37] without which we are spiritually dead.

Ḥadīth no.17

The Presence of the Angels when the Qur'ān is Recited

عَنْ مُحَمَّدِ بْنِ إِبْرَاهِيمَ عَنْ أُسَيْدِ بْنِ حُضَيْرٍ رَضِيَ اللَّهُ عَنْهُ، قَالَ:

بَيْنَمَا هُوَ يَقْرَأُ مِنَ اللَّيْلِ سُورَةَ الْبَقَرَةِ، وَفَرَسُهُ مَرْبُوطَةٌ عِنْدَهُ، إِذْ جَالَتِ الْفَرَسُ فَسَكَتَ فَسَكَتَتْ، فَقَرَأَ فَجَالَتِ الْفَرَسُ، فَسَكَتَ وَسَكَتَتِ الْفَرَسُ، ثُمَّ قَرَأَ فَجَالَتِ الْفَرَسُ فَانْصَرَفَ، وَكَانَ ابْنُهُ يَحْيَى قَرِيبًا مِنْهَا، فَأَشْفَقَ أَنْ تُصِيبَهُ فَلَمَّا اجْتَرَّهُ رَفَعَ رَأْسَهُ إِلَى السَّمَاءِ، حَتَّى مَا يَرَاهَا، فَلَمَّا أَصْبَحَ حَدَّثَ النَّبِيَّ صَلَّى اللَّهُ عَلَيْهِ وَسَلَّمَ فَقَالَ: اقْرَأْ يَا ابْنَ حُضَيْرٍ، اقْرَأْ يَا ابْنَ حُضَيْرٍ، قَالَ: فَأَشْفَقْتُ يَا رَسُولَ اللَّهِ أَنْ تَطَأَ يَحْيَى، وَكَانَ مِنْهَا قَرِيبًا، فَرَفَعْتُ رَأْسِي فَانْصَرَفْتُ إِلَيْهِ، فَرَفَعْتُ رَأْسِي إِلَى السَّمَاءِ، فَإِذَا مِثْلُ الظُّلَّةِ فِيهَا أَمْثَالُ الْمَصَابِيحِ، فَخَرَجَتْ حَتَّى لاَ أَرَاهَا، قَالَ: وَتَدْرِي مَا ذَاكَ؟، قَالَ: لاَ، قَالَ: تِلْكَ الْمَلاَئِكَةُ دَنَتْ لِصَوْتِكَ، وَلَوْ قَرَأْتَ لَأَصْبَحَتْ يَنْظُرُ النَّاسُ إِلَيْهَا، لاَ تَتَوَارَى مِنْهُمْ.

رَوَاهُ الْبُخَارِي

Muḥammad ibn Ibrāhīm رحمه الله narrated about Usaid bin Ḥuḍair رضي الله عنه states that while he was reciting Sūrah Al-Baqarah at night, with his horse tied beside him, the horse was suddenly startled and troubled. When he stopped reciting, the horse became quiet, and when he started again the horse was startled again. Then he stopped reciting and the horse became quiet too. He started reciting again and the horse was startled and troubled once again. Then he stopped reciting, for his son Yaḥyā was beside the horse and he was afraid that the horse might trample him. When he took the boy away and looked towards the sky, he could not see it. The next morning he informed the Prophet ﷺ who said, "You should have continued reciting, O Ibn Ḥuḍair! You should have continued reciting, O Ibn Ḥuḍair!" Ibn Ḥuḍair replied, "O Allāh's Messenger ﷺ! My son Yaḥyā was near the horse and I was afraid that it might trample him, so I looked towards the sky and went to him. When I looked at the sky I saw something like a cloud containing what looked like lamps, until it left and I could no longer see it." The Prophet ﷺ said, "Do you know what that was?" Ibn Ḥuḍair ؓ replied, "No." The Prophet ﷺ said, "Those were Angels who had drawn near to you due to your recitation, and had you kept on reciting until dawn, they would have remained there until morning, such that people would have seen them as they would not have disappeared."[38]

۞ This ḥadīth illustrates how the Angels love to hear the recitation of the Qur'ān, especially from those who recite the Qur'ān in a proficient and beautiful manner, since Usaid ؓ was known for having beautiful recitation.

۞ Some scholars stated that the home that has the Qur'ān recited in it illuminates for the inhabitants of the heavens, i.e. the Angels, just like the stars in the sky stand out for the people in this world.[39]

۞ Someone who recites the Qur'ān should remember this point when they recite the Qur'ān as it will help them to stay focused during the recitation and cherish it more.

۞ The ḥadīth also shows how it is possible for Angels to appear in physical forms in front of people, however, what is apparent is that they only do so in special circumstances.

Ḥadīth no.18

The Virtue of Reciting from the Muṣḥaf

عَنْ عَبْدِ اللهِ بن مَسْعُود رَضِيَ اللّٰهُ عَنْهُ قَالَ: قَالَ رَسُولُ اللهِ صَلَّى اللهُ عَلَيْهِ وَسَلَّمَ

مَنْ سَرَّهُ أَنْ يُحِبَّ اللّٰهَ وَرَسُولَهُ فَلْيَقْرَأْ فِي الْمُصْحَفِ

وَ فِي رِوَايَة: أَنْ يُحِبَّهُ اللّٰهُ.

رَوَاهُ أبو نعيم في حِلْيَةِ الأولياء

'Abdullāh Ibn Mas'ūd ؓ narrated that the Messenger of Allāh ﷺ said, "Whoever would like to be amongst those who love Allāh ﷻ and His Messenger, then let him read from the muṣḥaf." In another version it states, "Whoever would like Allāh ﷻ to love him..."[40]

- Whoever would like their love of Allāh ﷻ to increase should read from the *muṣḥaf*. By reading from the *muṣḥaf* a person engages their eyes in '*ibādah* as well as their tongue. This allows a person to focus more on what they are reciting as they are less likely to get visually distracted. Therefore, by engaging the heart, tongue and eyes, one is in a stronger position to draw closer to Allāh ﷻ.
- It is reported that many companions would dislike that a day should pass them by without them looking at the *muṣḥaf*.

Ḥadīth no.19

The Qur'ān Removes Sorrow and Anxiety

عَنْ عَبْدِ اللهِ بن مسعود رَضِيَ اللَّهُ عَنْهُ قَالَ: قَالَ رَسُولُ اللهِ صَلَّى اللهُ عَلَيْهِ وَسَلَّمَ:

مَا أَصَابَ أَحَدًا قَطُّ هَمٌّ وَلَا حَزَنٌ، فَقَالَ: اللهُمَّ إِنِّي عَبْدُكَ، ابْنُ عَبْدِكَ، ابْنُ أَمَتِكَ،نَاصِيَتِي بِيَدِكَ، مَاضٍ فِيَّ حُكْمُكَ، عَدْلٌ فِيَّ قَضَاؤُكَ، أَسْأَلُكَ بِكُلِّ اسْمٍ هُوَ لَكَ سَمَّيْتَ بِهِ نَفْسَكَ، أَوْ عَلَّمْتَهُ أَحَدًا مِنْ خَلْقِكَ، أَوْ أَنْزَلْتَهُ فِي كِتَابِكَ، أَوِ اسْتَأْثَرْتَ بِهِ فِي عِلْمِ الْغَيْبِ عِنْدَكَ، أَنْ تَجْعَلَ الْقُرْآنَ رَبِيعَ قَلْبِي، وَنُورَ صَدْرِي، وَجِلَاءَ حُزْنِي، وَذَهَابَ هَمِّي، إِلَّا أَذْهَبَ اللهُ هَمَّهُ وَحُزْنَهُ، وَأَبْدَلَهُ مَكَانَهُ فَرَحًا، قَالَ: فَقِيلَ: يَا رَسُولَ اللهِ، أَلَا نَتَعَلَّمُهَا؟ فَقَالَ: بَلَى، يَنْبَغِي لِمَنْ سَمِعَهَا أَنْ يَتَعَلَّمَهَا.

رَوَاهُ الإمام أحمد في المسند

'Abdullāh Ibn Mas'ūd ﷺ narrated that the Messenger of Allāh ﷺ said, "There is no-one who is afflicted by anxiety and grief, and says: 'Allāhumma inni 'abduka ibnu 'abdika ibnu amatika nāṣiyati bi yadika, māḍin fiyya hukmuka, 'adlun fiyya qaḍā'uka. As'aluka bi kulli ismin huwa laka sammayta bihi nafsaka aw 'allamtahu aḥadan min khalqika aw anzaltahu fi kitābika aw ista'tharta bihi fi 'ilmil-ghaybi 'indaka an taj'alal-Qur'āna rabī'a qalbi wa nūra ṣadri wa jilā' ḥuzni wa dhahāba hammi [O Allāh, I am Your slave, son of Your slave, son of Your female slave; my forelock is in Your hand, Your command over me is forever executed and Your decree over me is just. I ask You by every name belonging to You which You have named Yourself with, or You taught to any of Your creation, or revealed in Your Book, or You have preserved in the knowledge of the Unseen with You, that You make the Qur'ān the

Spring of my heart and the light of my breast, and a departure for my sorrow and a release for my anxiety],' but Allāh ﷻ will take away his anxiety and grief, and replace it with joy." He was asked, "O Messenger of Allāh ﷺ, should we learn this?" To which he said, "Of course; everyone who hears it should learn it."[41]

- The supplication begins by acknowledging one's own weak state and need for Allāh ﷻ which is a fundamental pillar of servitude (*'ubūdiyyah*), and then the greatness of Allāh ﷻ is mentioned.
- '*The Spring of my heart*' suggests a number of matters. Firstly, it implies that one's grief will be removed as people are generally happier during Spring, when the environment is more conducive for such feelings. Secondly, Spring is a time when the mercy of Allāh ﷻ becomes very apparent due to the revival of dead and barren land. Likewise, the Qur'ān gives life to the heart through the faith that it instils in an individual as well as other forms of beneficial knowledge.
- A person who is close to the Qur'ān understands the nature of the transient life that we live in, and so the problems of this life will always seem insignificant compared to what our true concerns should be.
- This supplication can be said in any language.

Ḥadīth no.20

The Qur'ān is a Light for the One Who Recites it

عَنْ أَبِي ذَرٍّ رَضِيَ اللهُ عَنْهُ قَالَ قُلْتُ:

يَا رَسُولَ اللهِ أَوْصِنِي قَالَ عَلَيْكَ بِتَقْوَى اللهِ فَإِنَّهُ رَأْسُ الأَمْرِ كُلِّهِ، قُلْتُ يَا رَسُولَ اللهِ
زِدْنِي قَالَ عَلَيْكَ بِتِلَاوَةِ القُرْآنِ فَإِنَّهُ نُورٌ لَكَ فِي الأَرْضِ وَذُخْرٌ لَكَ فِي السَّمَاءِ.

رواه ابن حبان في صحيحه

Abū Dharr narrated that he asked the Messenger of Allāh, "'O Messenger of Allāh, advise me.' He said, 'Hold fast to the taqwā of Allāh, for indeed, it is the peak of all affairs.' I then said, 'O Messenger of Allāh, advise me more.' He said, 'Hold fast to the recitation of the Qur'ān, for it will be a light for you on this earth and a treasure for you in the heavens.'"[42]

- The Qur'ān is a light for the believer as it guides us through darkness. As such, without the Qur'ān one will be in a state of darkness not knowing where they are or where they are going in life.
- In other versions of the ḥadīth, *dhikr* (remembrance) is mentioned instead of *dhukhr* (treasure). It is a treasure due to the immense reward for reciting it and it is a remembrance because the Angels make mention in the Heavens of those who read the Qur'ān.

Ḥadīth no.21

Allāh ﷻ Gives to those Preoccupied with the Qur'ān More than He does to those Who Call upon Him

عَنْ أَبِي سَعِيدٍ الخُدْرِيِّ رَضِيَ اللَّهُ عَنْهُ، قَالَ: قَالَ رَسُولُ اللَّهِ صَلَّى اللَّهُ عَلَيْهِ وَسَلَّمَ:

يَقُولُ الرَّبُّ عَزَّ وَجَلَّ: مَنْ شَغَلَهُ القُرْآنُ عَنْ ذِكْرِي وَمَسْأَلَتِي أَعْطَيْتُهُ أَفْضَلَ مَا أُعْطِي السَّائِلِينَ، وَفَضْلُ كَلَامِ اللَّهِ عَلَى سَائِرِ الكَلَامِ كَفَضْلِ اللَّهِ عَلَى خَلْقِهِ.

رَوَاهُ التِّرمِذِي

Abū Sa'īd al Khudri ﵁ reported that the Messenger of Allah ﷺ said, "The Lord, Blessed and Most High is He, has said: 'Whoever is too preoccupied with the Qur'ān to make dhikr of Me and asking Me, then I shall give him more than what I give to those who ask.' And the superiority of Allah's ﷻ speech over the speech of others is like the superiority of Allāh ﷻ over His creation."[43]

- Preoccupying one's time with the Qur'ān means to read, memorise, reflect over its meanings and act upon its dictates.
- It should not be assumed however that a person should reduce in making *du'ā* to Allāh ﷻ in order for their supplications to be answered. Rather, the ḥadīth teaches us that we should not just approach Allāh ﷻ when we have needs to be seen to. The believer is someone who loves to worship Allāh ﷻ and study His words. Allāh ﷻ loves those who do not simply restrict their relationship with Allāh ﷻ to a matter of asking and taking. Hence, the closer a servant is to Allāh ﷻ, the more He will shower them with His grace.
- The second part of the narration '*And the superiority of Allāh...*' seems to be from the Prophet ﷺ himself. It can be viewed as being a reason

behind the initial statement, i.e. because Allāh's ﷻ speech is so superior it surpasses all other forms of remembrance.

- When reciting the Qur'ān a person should strive to recall that these are the very words that Allāh ﷻ spoke.

Ḥadīth no.22

The Virtue of Reciting the Qur'ān at Night while in Prayer

عَنْ عَبْدِ اللَّهِ بْنِ عَمْرِو بْنِ الْعَاصِ رَضِيَ اللَّهُ عَنْهُ قَالَ قَالَ رَسُولُ اللَّهِ صَلَّى اللهُ عَلَيْهِ وَسَلَّمَ:

مَنْ قَامَ بِعَشْرِ آيَاتٍ لَمْ يُكْتَبْ مِنَ الْغَافِلِينَ وَمَنْ قَامَ بِمِائَةِ آيَةٍ كُتِبَ مِنَ الْقَانِتِينَ وَمَنْ قَامَ بِأَلْفِ آيَةٍ كُتِبَ مِنَ الْمُقَنْطِرِينَ.

رَوَاهُ أَبُو دَاوُد

'Abdullāh ibn 'Amr ibn al 'Āṣ ؓ narrated that the Prophet ﷺ said, "If anyone prays at night reciting ten verses, he will not be recorded among the heedless; if anyone prays at night and recites a hundred verses, he will be recorded among those who are obedient to Allah; and if anyone prays at night reciting one thousand verses, he will be recorded among those who receive huge rewards."[44]

- The phrase '*man qāma*' is an indirect expression that refers to someone who memorises, recites and reflects over the meanings of those verses and acts upon them. Such a person will not be heedless in nature due to the connection they have with the Qur'ān. It was also said that such a person's name will not be written in the records of the heedless.
- Reciting the Qur'ān at any time during the day is virtuous, but it is especially virtuous at night while in prayer. Allāh ﷻ says, "*Truly the ris-*

ing by night is most potent for governing [the soul] and most suitable for [framing] the Word [of Prayer and Praise]."[45]

❂ It is widely accepted that one of the best methods to help a person memorise and revise the Qur'ān is by reciting it in night prayers. This is especially true when a person does so with repetition and contemplation.

Ḥadīth no.23

The Devil Flees from the Home where Sûrah al Baqarah is Recited

عَنْ أَبِي هُرَيْرَةَ رَضِيَ اللهُ عَنْهُ أَنَّ رَسُولَ اللهِ صَلَّى اللهُ عَلَيْهِ وَسَلَّمَ قَالَ:

لا تَجْعَلُوا بُيُوتَكُمْ مَقَابِرَ إِنَّ الشَّيْطَانَ يَفِرُّ مِنَ الْبَيْتِ الَّذِي تُقْرَأُ فِيهِ سُورَةُ الْبَقَرَةِ.

رَوَاهُ مُسْلِم

Abū Hurairah ﷺ reported that Allāh's Messenger ﷺ said, "Do not make your houses as graveyards for Satan runs away from the house in which Sūrah al Baqarah is recited."[46]

❂ Do not make your homes devoid of remembrance, recitation of the Qur'ān and acts of obedience or they will be like graveyards, since the dead cannot perform any good deeds.

❂ People who do not engage in those acts of worship are likened to the dead.

❂ *Sūrah al Baqarah* has been singled out due its multiple blessings and features: its length, the numerous times Allāh ﷻ is mentioned and the great many rulings provided in it. It is said that it contains 1,000 commandments, prohibitions, rulings, and information about past and future events. It also exposes the traits of the *Shayṭān*, depicts many miracles, exhortations and attributes of the righteous.

Ḥadīth no.24

Contemplating the Words of Allāh ﷻ

قَالَ ابْنُ عُمَيْرٍ رَضِيَ اللَّهُ عَنْهُ لِعَائِشَةَ رَضِيَ اللهُ عَنْهَا:

أَخْبِرِينَا بِأَعْجَبِ شَيْءٍ رَأَيْتِهِ مِنْ رَسُولِ اللَّهِ صَلَّى اللَّهُ عَلَيْهِ وَسَلَّمَ، قَالَ: فَسَكَتَتْ ثُمَّ قَالَتْ: لَمَّا كَانَ لَيْلَةٌ مِنَ اللَّيَالِي، قَالَ: يَا عَائِشَةُ ذَرِينِي أَتَعَبَّدُ اللَّيْلَةَ لِرَبِّي قُلْتُ: وَاللَّهِ إِنِّي لَأُحِبُّ قُرْبَكَ، وَأُحِبُّ مَا سَرَّكَ، قَالَتْ: فَقَامَ فَتَطَهَّرَ، ثُمَّ قَامَ يُصَلِّي، قَالَتْ: فَلَمْ يَزَلْ يَبْكِي حَتَّى بَلَّ حِجْرَهُ، قَالَتْ: ثُمَّ بَكَى فَلَمْ يَزَلْ يَبْكِي حَتَّى بَلَّ لِحْيَتَهُ، قَالَتْ: ثُمَّ بَكَى فَلَمْ يَزَلْ يَبْكِي حَتَّى بَلَّ الْأَرْضَ، فَجَاءَ بِلَالٌ يُؤْذِنُهُ بِالصَّلَاةِ، فَلَمَّا رَآهُ يَبْكِي، قَالَ: يَا رَسُولَ اللَّهِ، لِمَ تَبْكِي وَقَدْ غَفَرَ اللَّهُ لَكَ مَا تَقَدَّمَ وَمَا تَأَخَّرَ؟، قَالَ: أَفَلَا أَكُونُ عَبْدًا شَكُورًا، لَقَدْ نَزَلَتْ عَلَيَّ اللَّيْلَةَ آيَةٌ، وَيْلٌ لِمَنْ قَرَأَهَا وَلَمْ يَتَفَكَّرْ فِيهَا {إِنَّ فِي خَلْقِ ٱلسَّمَٰوَٰتِ وَٱلْأَرْضِ وَٱخْتِلَٰفِ ٱلَّيْلِ وَٱلنَّهَارِ لَءَايَٰتٍ لِّأُو۟لِى ٱلْأَلْبَٰبِ ﴿١٩٠﴾} [آل عمران: ١٩٠].

رَوَاهُ ابنُ حِبَّان في صَحِيحِه

Ibn 'Umair ﷺ said to 'Ā'ishah ﷺ, "Inform us of the most amazing thing you have seen from the Prophet ﷺ." She was quiet for a moment and then said, "During one night he ﷺ said to me: 'O 'Ā'ishah, let me worship my Lord this night' so I replied, 'By Allāh ﷻ, I love being close to you but I also love that which pleases you.' She said, "Then he ﷺ stood and made ablution to pray" She said, "He continued to cry until his tears wet his lap. Then he cried until his beard was soaked with tears. He continued to cry until the floor became wet with his tears.

Bilāl ⚅ then came asking permission to call for prayer, but when he saw the Prophet ⚅ crying he said, 'O Messenger of Allāh, why do you cry when Allāh ⚅ has forgiven all of your past and future sins?' He ⚅ said, 'Should I not be a grateful servant? A verse has been revealed to me this night; Woe to the one who reads it and does not reflect over its meanings: **Indeed, in the creation of the heavens and the earth and the alternation of the night and the day are signs for those of understanding.** *(3:190)"* [47]

⚙ The Qur'ān was revealed for reflection and to act upon. Allāh ⚅ said, "*[This is] a blessed Book which We have revealed to you, [O Muhammad], that they might reflect upon its verses and that those of understanding would be reminded.*" (38:29)

⚙ Anas bin Mālik ⚅ said, "Perhaps one is reciting the Qur'ān and the Qur'ān is cursing him."[48] This should not discourage a person from reading the Qur'ān since it is not the recitation that will be against the reciter; rather, it is their inaction that is blameworthy.

⚙ Contemplation (*tadabbur*), linguistically means to "reflect over the consequences or results (*'āqibah*) of a matter and to ponder over it."[49] Technically, it means to attempt to perceive what lies behind the intended meaning in terms of guidance and instruction. In order to achieve this a person has to have an active mind when reading and has to consciously question themselves as to what guidance can be derived from what they are reading. Sufyān ibn 'Uyaynah ⚅ said, "The verses of the Qur'ān are like treasure houses. Therefore, if you enter one, strive to make sure that you do not leave it unless you have discovered some of the treasure."[50]

⚙ The aforementioned points should encourage a person to strive and reflect over the meanings of the Qur'ān.

Ḥadīth no.25

Honouring the Bearer of the Qur'ān is Veneration of Allāh ﷻ

عَنْ أَبِي مُوسَى الأَشْعَرِيِّ رَضِيَ اللَّهُ عَنْهُ قَالَ قَالَ رَسُولُ اللَّهِ -صَلَّى اللهُ عَلَيْهِ وَسَلَّمَ:

إِنَّ مِنْ إِجْلاَلِ اللَّهِ إِكْرَامَ ذِى الشَّيْبَةِ الْمُسْلِمِ وَحَامِلِ الْقُرْآنِ غَيْرِ الْغَالِى فِيهِ وَالْجَافِى عَنْهُ وَإِكْرَامَ ذِى السُّلْطَانِ الْمُقْسِطِ.

رواهُ أبو داوُد

Abū Mūsa al-Ash'ari ؓ narrated that the Prophet ﷺ said, "Venerating Allāh ﷻ involves showing honour to a grey-haired Muslim and to the bearer of the Qur'ān, not to one who acts extravagantly regarding it, or turns away from it, and [it involves] showing honour to a just ruler."[51]

- One of the ways of venerating Allāh ﷻ is by honouring such people due to the status they have with Allāh ﷻ.
- The elderly have a virtue of possessing faith for a longer period of time compared to those younger, and thus have accumulated many good deeds.
- As for the bearers of the Qur'ān, they deserve to be honoured because they carry the words of Allāh ﷻ in their hearts.
- The Prophet ﷺ stipulated two matters. The first is that a person should not act extravagantly towards the Qur'ān. This can be done by looking for hidden meanings or by exaggerating in the pronunciation of letters. The second is by abandoning the recitation and reflection of the Qur'ān and no longer acting upon it.
- Another possible understanding of this ḥadīth is that Allāh ﷻ venerates such people such as the elderly and the bearer of the Qur'ān, by honouring them.

Ḥadīth no.26

Reciting the Qur'ān by one Who is More Skilled to one Who is Inferior to him, and the Excellence of the People of the Qur'ān

عَنْ أَنَسِ بْنِ مَالِكٍ رَضِيَ اللَّهُ عَنْهُ، قَالَ النَّبِيُّ صَلَّى اللهُ عَلَيْهِ وَسَلَّمَ لِأُبَيٍّ:

إِنَّ اللَّهَ أَمَرَنِي أَنْ أَقْرَأَ عَلَيْكَ {لَمْ يَكُنِ ٱلَّذِينَ كَفَرُواْ مِنْ أَهْلِ ٱلْكِتَٰبِ}

[البينة: ١] قَالَ: وَسَمَّانِي؟ قَالَ: «نَعَمْ» فَبَكَى.

رواه البُخاري

Anas bin Mālik ﷺ narrated that the Prophet ﷺ said to Ubayy bin Ka'b ﷺ, "Allāh has ordered me to recite to you: Those who disbelieve among the people of the Scripture and among the polytheists are not going to stop [their disbelief]. (98:1)" Ubayy ﷺ said, "Did Allāh ﷻ mention me by name?" The Prophet ﷺ said, "Yes" On that, Ubayy ﷺ wept.[52]

- Imam al-Nawawi رحمه الله commentates on the ḥadīth, saying, "This ḥadīth has a number of benefits. It is recommended to recite the Qur'ān to expert reciters and those knowledgeable of it even if the reciter is more virtuous than the one who he is reciting to."
- The ḥadīth also establishes the virtue of Ubayy ﷺ as the Prophet ﷺ recited the Qur'ān to him, and it is not known if anyone shared this virtue with Ubayy ﷺ. The Prophet ﷺ said about him, "The most proficient of you with regards to the Qur'ān is Ubayy ﷺ."
- His virtue is also established by the fact that Allāh ﷻ mentioned him by name. Both virtues are as a result of the status he had for being from the people of the Qur'ān.
- The scholars gave various possible answers as to why the Prophet

was ordered to recite to someone. Al Nawawi opined that it was done in order to teach the *ummah* the virtue of reciting the Qur'ān to those who have perfected its recitation. It was also said that this was done in order to acknowledge the virtue of Ubayy and to confirm that he was qualified to convey the Qur'ān directly from the Prophet in a masterful manner. Hence, it is of no surprise that countless people learnt the Qur'ān from Ubayy for many years thereafter.

❂ Ubayy cried either out of happiness that Allāh mentioned him by name or out of fear of not being able to reciprocate such a huge blessing with sufficient gratitude.

Ḥadīth no.27

The Virtue of Being Consistent in the Recitation of the Qur'ān and the Danger of Not Being Consistent in it

عَنْ أَبِي مُوسَى رَضِيَ اللَّهُ عَنْهُ، عَنِ النَّبِيِّ صَلَّى اللَّهُ عَلَيْهِ وَسَلَّمَ، قَالَ:

تَعَاهَدُوا هَذَا الْقُرْآنَ، فَوَالَّذِي نَفْسُ مُحَمَّدٍ بِيَدِهِ لَهُوَ أَشَدُّ تَفَلُّتًا مِنَ الْإِبِلِ فِي عُقُلِهَا.

رواهُ مُسلم

Abū Mūsa reported that the Prophet said, "Recite the Qur'ān regularly, for, by Him in Whose Hand is my life, the Qur'ān escapes one's memory faster than camels that are released from their tying ropes."[53]

❂ By being consistent in reciting the Qur'ān, a person is capable of retaining what they have memorised.

❂ If the *ḥuffāẓ* of the Qur'ān do not revise regularly they will inevitably forget what they have memorised. Hence, most teachers of the Qur'ān stress on revision more so than memorisation itself. Moreover, some experts of the Qur'ān recommend that a *ḥāfiẓ* revise between 1-3 *juz'* on a daily basis.

۞ Another way of maintaining the Qur'ān is by acting upon it. The scholars say, "Hold onto knowledge by acting upon it."

Ḥadīth no.28

The Virtue of Repeating Verses

عَنْ جَسْرَةَ بِنْتِ دَجَاجَةَ ، قَالَتْ : سَمِعْتُ أَبَا ذَرٍّ، يَقُولُ :

قَامَ النَّبِيُّ صَلَّى اللهُ عَلَيْهِ وَسَلَّمَ بِآيَةٍ حَتَّى أَصْبَحَ يُرَدِّدُهَا وَالْآيَةُ : {إِن تُعَذِّبْهُمْ فَإِنَّهُمْ عِبَادُكَ ۖ وَإِن تَغْفِرْ لَهُمْ فَإِنَّكَ أَنتَ ٱلْعَزِيزُ ٱلْحَكِيمُ ﴿١١٨﴾} [المائدة : ١١٨].

رواهُ ابنُ ماجه

Jasrah bint Dajājah said, "I heard Abu Dharr ﷺ say, 'The Prophet ﷺ stood reciting a verse and repeated it until morning came. That verse was: If you punish them – indeed they are Your slaves; and if You forgive them - verily You, only You, are the All-Mighty, the All-Wise. (5:118)'"[a54]

۞ Repeating verses helps one to ponder and reflect over their meanings.

۞ This supplication was originally said by *'Īsā* ﷺ. However, it seems the Prophet ﷺ was using the same supplication for his *ummah*.

۞ When we read the supplications of other Prophets in the Qur'ān we should emulate them in making the same supplication, and not just read the verse as though it is merely narrating an incident.

۞ There are numerous reports that indicate that this was the practice of the companions and the early generations. Ibn al Qayyim ﷺ said, "This was the practice of the Salaf; they would repeat a verse until the morning."[55]

۞ Al Ḥasan al Baṣri ﷺ repeated the following verse until the morning: *And if you were to count the blessings of your Lord, you would not be able to enumerate them.* (14:34) He was asked why he did that and he replied, "We do not lay our gaze on something or look away from something except that our sights fall upon a blessing of Allāh ﷻ. However, despite that, the blessings of Allāh ﷻ are more than we can ever know."[56]

Rulings

related to the Qur'ān

aḥādīth 29-40

Ḥadīth no.29

Seeking Refuge in Allāh ﷻ Before Reciting

عَنْ أَبِي سَعِيدٍ الْخُدْرِيِّ رَضِيَ اللَّهُ عَنْهُ قَالَ:

كَانَ رَسُولُ اللَّهِ صَلَّى اللهُ عَلَيْهِ وَسَلَّمَ إِذَا قَامَ مِنَ اللَّيْلِ كَبَّرَ ثُمَّ يَقُولُ سُبْحَانَكَ اللَّهُمَّ وَبِحَمْدِكَ وَتَبَارَكَ اسْمُكَ وَتَعَالَى جَدُّكَ وَلاَ إِلَهَ غَيْرُكَ. ثُمَّ يَقُولُ لاَ إِلَهَ إِلاَّ اللَّهُ. ثَلاَثًا ثُمَّ يَقُولُ اللَّهُ أَكْبَرُ كَبِيرًا. ثَلاَثًا أَعُوذُ بِاللَّهِ السَّمِيعِ الْعَلِيمِ مِنَ الشَّيْطَانِ الرَّجِيمِ مِنْ هَمْزِهِ وَنَفْخِهِ وَنَفْثِهِ. ثُمَّ يَقْرَأُ.

رواهُ أبو داود

Abū Sa'īd al Khudri ﷺ reported that when the Messenger of Allāh ﷺ got up to pray at night, he uttered the takbīr and then said, 'Glory be to Thee, O Allāh, Praise be to Thee, Blessed is Thy name, Exalted is Thy greatness and There is no god but Thee.' He then said, 'There is no god but Allāh' three times. Then he said 'Allāh is the greatest' three times [and] 'I seek refuge in Allāh, All-Hearing and All-Knowing from the accursed shayṭān, from his evil suggestion (hamz),[57] from pride (nafkh), and from his magic and poetry (nafth).' He then recited [the Qur'ān]."[58]

- Allāh ﷻ says, "*So when you recite the Qur'ān, [first] seek refuge in Allāh from Shayṭān, the expelled [from His mercy].*"[59]
- Due to the immense reward gained from reading the Qur'ān, the Shayṭān strives to deter and distract a person seeking to read it. We should be conscious of this challenge every time we read the Qur'ān.
- Seeking refuge in Allāh ﷻ is not merely an utterance. It is primarily an action of the heart and thereafter an utterance.
- Ibn al Qayyim رحمه الله explains the reality of seeking refuge in Allāh ﷻ

to be "fleeing from something that you fear to someone who will protect you from it."[60]

- There are different versions of the *isti'ādhah* (the invocation that is said to seek refuge in Allāh ﷻ) one can use:
    - *A'ūthu billāhi-minash-Shayṭānir-rajīm.*
    - *A'ūthu billāhis-Samī'il 'Alīm minash-Shayṭānir-rajīm*
    - *A'ūthu billāhis-Samī'il 'Alīm minash-Shayṭānir-rajīm min hamzihi wa nafkhihi wa nafthihi*
    - *A'ūthu billāhil-'Aẓīm wa bi-wajhihil Karīm wa sulṭānihil-qadīm minash-Shayṭānir-rajīm*
- The *isti'ādhah* should be said aloud if one is reciting aloud. However, during prayer it should be said quietly.
- If a person's recitation is interrupted by something out of their control like sneezing or yawning, then this person does not need to repeat the *isti'ādhah*. However, if they interrupt their recitation voluntarily, such as in replying to someone's speech or greeting, then they should repeat the *isti'ādhah*.[61]

Ḥadīth no.30

Only the Ritually Pure Should Touch the Qur'ān

عَنْ عَبْدِ اللهِ بْنِ أَبِي بَكْرِ بْنِ حَزْمٍ رَضِيَ اللهُ عَنْهُ؛

أَنَّ فِي الْكِتَابِ الَّذِي كَتَبَهُ رَسُولُ اللهِ ﷺ لِعَمْرِو بْنِ حَزْمٍ: أَنْ لاَ يَمَسَّ الْقُرْآنَ إِلاَّ طَاهِرٌ.

رَوَاهُ الإِمَامُ مَالِكٌ فِي المُوَطَّأ

'Abdullah bin Abī Bakr bin Ḥazm ؓ narrated that it was written in the Prophet's ﷺ letter to 'Amr bin Ḥazm ؓ that "No one should touch the Qur'ān except a person who is pure."[62]

- The *muṣḥaf* deserves great veneration and respect. As a result of this there are many rulings and etiquettes dealing with how we must treat the book of Allāh ﷻ.
- The term *ṭāhir* (pure) can convey a number of meanings:
  - Figuratively pure, i.e. pure from *shirk*. Allāh ﷻ says, "*O you who have believed, indeed the polytheists are unclean...*"[61]
  - Pure from physical impurities.
  - Purity in a ritual sense. This means to be pure from major and minor states of spiritual impurity.
- The meaning of *ṭāhir* here is the one who has removed their state of impurity through ablution, i.e. *mutawaḍḍi'*. This is apparent as the term *ṭāhir* is predominately used in the *sharī'ah* to refer to someone in a ritual state of purity.
- Allāh ﷻ says, "*None touch it except the purified.*"[64] Although some scholars held this to refer to the Angels with respect to the Sacred Tablet (*al Lawḥ al Maḥfūẓ*), it still can be used to refer to the prohibition of touching the *muṣḥaf* in this world since if only the Angels are allowed to touch the Sacred Tablet, then only the pure amongst us should be

allowed to touch the *muṣḥaf.*

- This is the opinion of the majority of the companions, their successors and also the view of the four Imams. Ibn Qudāmah ﷺ said, "We do not know of an opposing view to this other than the view of Dāwūd (al Ẓāhiri)."[65]
- It is not permissible to touch the pages of the *muṣḥaf*, margins and cover without *wuḍū'*.
- It is permissible to carry the *muṣḥaf* if it is wrapped by an external cover or straps since the prohibition is related to touching the *muṣḥaf* directly.
- It is permissible to touch books of *tafsīr* or *ḥadīth* that contain verses of the Qur'ān without *wuḍū'* as the majority of the text is not from the Qur'ān, and therefore does not take the ruling of the *muṣḥaf.* Likewise, it is permissible to touch 'translations' of the Qur'ān without *wuḍū'*.
- If an electronic device such as a smart phone or tablet displays the Qur'ān it is better to avoid touching it without *wuḍū'*. When they are not displaying the Qur'ān, being in a state of *wuḍū'* is not necessary.

Ḥadīth no.31

Can the Sexually Impure or Menstruating Women recite the Qur'ān?

عَنِ ابْنِ عُمَرَ عَنِ رَضِيَ اللهُ عَنْهُ النَّبِيِّ صَلَّى اللهُ عَلَيْهِ وَسَلَّمَ قَالَ:

لَا تَقْرَأِ الحَائِضُ، وَلَا الجُنُبُ شَيْئًا مِنَ القُرْآنِ.

رَوَاهُ التِّرْمِذِي

Ibn 'Umar narrated that the Prophet said, "The ḥā'iḍ (menstruating woman) and the junub (one in a state of sexual impurity) should not recite anything from the Qur'ān."[66]

- Although the authenticity of this ḥadīth is disputed, most scholars cite it as proof for the prohibition of reciting the Qur'ān for the *junub* and *ḥā'iḍ* as there is substantial supporting evidence for this.
- Sexual impurity (*janābah*) occurs due to intercourse (whether there is ejaculation or not), ejaculation and wet dreams.
- According to the majority of the four schools of thought, *Ḥanafi*, *Shāfi'ī* and *Ḥanbali*, it is prohibited for the *ḥā'iḍ* to recite the Qur'ān aloud from memory. The *Māliki* school of thought as well as some scholars like Ibn Taymiyyah held the view that it is permissible for the *ḥā'iḍ* to recite the Qur'ān from memory.
- After citing this ḥadīth, Imām al Tirmidhi said, "This is the view of most of the people of knowledge from the companions of the Prophet, the successors and those who came after them like: Sufyān al Thawri, Ibn al Mubārak, al Shāfi'ī, Aḥmad and Isḥāq. They all said that it is not permissible for the menstruating woman or the *junub* to recite anything from the Qur'ān except for a part of a verse or some letters or words. However, they are allowed to make *tasbīḥ* and *tahlīl* (to say *lā ilāha*

illallāh)."[67] That is, to make *dhikr*.

✪ An argument that is used against this *ḥadīth* is that it is not conceivable that a woman not be allowed to recite the Qur'ān for a long period of time, as she may forget portions of what she has memorised. However, it is the agreement of the scholars that a *ḥā'iḍ* cannot pray during menstruation. Prayer is the most important act of worship that a person can perform and through prayer they are closest to their Lord. And yet, despite this, it is not permitted for a *ḥā'iḍ* to pray. If such is the case with regards to *ṣalāh*, then why is it inconceivable that a woman not be permitted to recite the Qur'ān during menstruation?

✪ A *ḥā'iḍ* can still listen to the Qur'ān and revise it in her mind. Likewise, if she is a Qur'ān teacher she can use electronic applications and devices to assist in her teaching.

Ḥadīth no.32

The Importance of Reciting the Qur'ān with a Melodious Voice

عن أَبِي هُرَيْرَةَ رَضِيَ اللَّهُ عَنْهُ، قَالَ قَالَ رَسُولُ اللهِ صَلَّى اللهُ عَلَيْهِ وَسَلَّمَ:

لَيْسَ مِنَّا مَنْ لَمْ يَتَغَنَّ بِالْقُرْآنِ.

رَوَاهُ الْبُخَارِي

Abū Hurayrah ؓ narrated that the Messenger of Allāh ﷺ said, "Whoever does not recite the Qur'ān with a melodious voice is not from us."[68]

✪ The recitation of the Qur'ān should be done in a beautiful manner with a sense of awe (*khushū'*) in order to venerate the words of Allāh ﷻ and to facilitate contemplation (tadabbur) of His words.

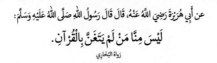

❂ '*Taghanni*' has been interpreted in number of ways. According to one understanding it refers to beautifying one's voice (*taḥsīn al ṣawt*). Another understanding is that it refers to sufficing oneself through the Qur'ān. It is reported that Ibn Mas'ūd said, "Whoever reads *Āl 'Imrān* is prosperous (*ghaniyy*)."[69] A third understanding, which is attributed to Imām al Shāfi'ī ﷺ, is that it refers to reciting with a sense of sadness (*taḥazzun*) and with melody (*tarannum*).

❂ One has to be careful to observe sincerity when attempting to beautify one's voice and not make the beautification an objective in and of itself. As for copying musical tones, such as the various *maqāmāt* that many people are becoming infatuated with today, it has no precedence from the heritage of our reciters and in many ways it is distracting people from reflecting and acting upon the Qur'ān.

❂ One should not compromise the rules of *tajwīd* in order to beautify their recitation.

Ḥadīth no.33

Reciting According to the Way of the Prophet ﷺ

عَنْ قَتَادَةَ، قَالَ:

سُئِلَ أَنَسٌ كَيْفَ كَانَتْ قِرَاءَةُ النَّبِيِّ صَلَّى اللهُ عَلَيْهِ وَسَلَّمَ؟ فَقَالَ: كَانَتْ مَدًّا، ثُمَّ قَرَأَ: {بِسۡمِ ٱللَّهِ ٱلرَّحۡمَٰنِ ٱلرَّحِيمِ} يَمُدُّ بِبِسْمِ اللَّهِ، وَيَمُدُّ بِالرَّحْمَنِ، وَيَمُدُّ بِالرَّحِيمِ.

رواه البخاري

Qatādah رحمه الله *said, "Anas* رضي الله عنه *was asked, 'How was the recitation of the Prophet* ﷺ*?' He replied, 'It was characterised by the lengthening of certain sounds.' He then recited 'bismillāh al Raḥmān al Raḥīm', lengthening the pronunciation of bismillāh, al Raḥmān, and al Raḥīm."*[70]

- One should learn to recite the Qur'ān well, just like the Prophet ﷺ did with *tajwīd*. Literally, *tajwīd* means to do something well. Technically, it refers to the correct pronunciation of letters and to giving them their due rights. *Tajwīd* is not restricted to the pronunciation of letters, but also of words, phrases and sentences. The *tajwīd* of words refers to observing rulings pertaining to how to connect letters and words with other letters and words (e.g *iẓhār, idghām, ikhfā'* and *iqlāb*) as well as observing the lengthening of letters (*mudūd*). The *tajwīd* of sentences refers to observing the correct places to start and stop one's recitation.
- Observing the rules of *tajwīd* is considered to be a form of veneration of Allāh's words; hence, a person should strive to learn its rules. Many scholars considered that learning *tajwīd* and putting it into practice is a religious obligation, otherwise a person will make mistakes and potentially change the meaning of what they recite.

Ḥadīth no.34

The Prostration of Recitation

عَنْ أَبِي هُرَيْرَةَ رَضِيَ اللَّهُ عَنْهُ، قَالَ: قَالَ رَسُولُ اللهِ صَلَّى اللهُ عَلَيْهِ وَسَلَّمَ:

إِذَا قَرَأَ ابْنُ آدَمَ السَّجْدَةَ فَسَجَدَ اعْتَزَلَ الشَّيْطَانُ يَبْكِي، يَقُولُ: يَا وَيْلَهُ - وَفِي رِوَايَةِ أَبِي كُرَيْبٍ: يَا وَيْلِي - أُمِرَ ابْنُ آدَمَ بِالسُّجُودِ فَسَجَدَ فَلَهُ الْجَنَّةُ، وَأُمِرْتُ بِالسُّجُودِ فَأَبَيْتُ فَلِيَ النَّارُ.

رَواهُ مُسلِم

Abū Hurairah ﷺ said that the Prophet ﷺ said, "When the son of Ādam recites an āyah of sajdah (prostration) and then falls down in prostration, Satan goes into seclusion and weeps and says, 'Alas'. [In the narration of Abū Kuraib ﷺ the words are: 'Woe unto me,] the son of Ādam was commanded to prostrate and he prostrated, and Paradise was entitled to him. And I was commanded to prostrate but I refused and am doomed to Hell.'"[71]

۞ Refusing to prostrate is a sign of arrogance and pride. Hence, the prostration is a sign of humility and obedience.

۞ This ḥadīth is cited by some scholars, such as the *aḥnāf*, as proof of the obligation of prostrating when reciting or listening to a verse of prostration. The majority, however, hold it to be recommended and not obligatory, as it was once reported that *Sūrah al Najm* was recited to the Prophet ﷺ and yet he did not prostrate upon listening to the verse of prostration in it.[72]

۞ The prostration should be performed by the one who intentionally listens to the recitation and not the one who merely hears it being recited.

⚙ According to the majority of scholars the prostration is considered to be a type of *ṣalāh* and so the same conditions of *ṣalāh* apply to it, such as the condition of purity. Some scholars such as Imām al Bukhāri رَحِمَهُ اللّٰه and Ibn Taymiyyah رَحِمَهُ اللّٰه were of the view that these conditions are not stipulated as there are too many differences between the prostration and the prayer itself to make an analogy between the two. However, they were of the view that these conditions are advisable to follow.

⚙ The prostration is done in prayer and outside of prayer. If done in prayer, one should say the *takbīr* and descend into prostration.

⚙ The manner of performing it outside of prayer is as follows:

   ◉ *Takbīr*: many scholars say one should say the *takbīr* when descending into prostration and rising from it.

   ◉ Standing: the scholars differed about whether a person should stand up straight before going into prostration. There is a report that mentions that 'Ā'ishah رَضِيَ اللّٰهُ عَنْها used to stand up before prostrating but it seems to be a weak narration,[73] as mentioned by al Nawawi رَحِمَهُ اللّٰه.[74]

   ◉ A person can say what they usually say in prostration but they can also add: "*sajada wajhi lilladhī khalqahu wa shaqqa sam'ahu wa baṣarahu bi ḥawlihi wa quwwatihi*"

   ◉ *Taslīm*: this is disputed more than the aforementioned issues. The view of the *aḥnāf*, one view of the *shāfi'iyyah*, the well-known opinion of the *mālikiyyah* and an opinion of the *ḥanābilah* is that there is no *taslīm* at the end. Otherwise, the main view of the *shāfi'iyyah* and the *ḥanābilah* and the other view of the *mālikiyyah* is that one should do the *taslīm* as the prostration is a type of prayer and thus should end like a prayer.

Ḥadīth no.35

Speculative Argumentation over the Qur'ān is Disbelief

عَنْ أَبِي هُرَيْرَةَ رَضِيَ اللَّهُ عَنْهُ، عَنِ النَّبِيِّ صَلَّى اللهُ عَلَيْهِ وَسَلَّمَ قَالَ:

الْمِرَاءُ فِي الْقُرْآنِ كُفْرٌ.

رَوَاهُ أبو داود

Abū Hurayrah reported that the Prophet said, "Speculative argumentation about the Qur'ān is kufr."[75]

- Delving into arguments about the Qur'ān without sound knowledge is totally prohibited as it can lead to the rejection of verses and other established tenants.
- Some scholars were of the view that the word '*mirā*' in the ḥadīth refers to doubt, i.e. doubting the Qur'ān leads to disbelief.
- In some cases people speculate over certain verses and its teachings because they approach the Qur'ān with preconceived ideas of what is right and wrong and so measure up the Qur'ān in light of that. A person should not approach the Qur'ān in such a manner. Instead, we should allow the Qur'ān to state what is right and wrong and accuse our own understanding before doubting the teachings of the Qur'ān.

Ḥadīth no.36

How Often Should One Recite the Qur'ān?

عَنْ عَبْدِ اللَّهِ بْنِ عَمْرٍو، قَالَ: قَالَ رَسُولُ اللَّهِ صَلَّى اللهُ عَلَيْهِ وَسَلَّمَ

اقْرَإِ الْقُرْآنَ فِي شَهْرٍ" قُلْتُ: إِنِّي أَجِدُ قُوَّةً حَتَّى قَالَ: "فَاقْرَأْهُ فِي سَبْعٍ وَلاَ تَزِدْ عَلَى ذَلِكَ.

رَوَاهُ الْبُخَارِي

'Abdullāh bin 'Amr ؓ said, "Allāh's Messenger ﷺ said to me, 'Recite the whole Qur'ān in one month.' I said, 'But I have the ability [to do more than that].' Allāh's Messenger ﷺ said, 'Then finish the recitation of the Qur'ān in seven days, and do not finish it in less than this period.'"[76]

- The companions possessed a great deal of eagerness to complete reading the Qur'ān over and over again.
- There is no fixed sunnah for how often a person should complete the Qur'ān as that will differ from person to person depending upon one's ability to comprehend what they recite. The fact that the Prophet ﷺ began advising with one month and then went down to seven days indicates this.
- It is recommended to recite it as often as possible on condition that one can understand what they are reciting, thereby combining the virtue of measured recitation with understanding of what one recites.

Ḥadīth no.37

Reciting the Qur'ān with Meaning and Supplicating During its Recitation

عَنْ حُذَيْفَةَ رَضِيَ اللهُ عَنْهُ، قَالَ:

صَلَّيْتُ مَعَ النَّبِيِّ صَلَّى اللهُ عَلَيْهِ وَسَلَّمَ ذَاتَ لَيْلَةٍ، فَافْتَتَحَ الْبَقَرَةَ، فَقُلْتُ: يَرْكَعُ عِنْدَ
الْمِائَةِ، ثُمَّ مَضَى، فَقُلْتُ: يُصَلِّي بِهَا فِي رَكْعَةٍ، فَمَضَى، فَقُلْتُ: يَرْكَعُ بِهَا، ثُمَّ افْتَتَحَ
النِّسَاءَ، فَقَرَأَهَا، ثُمَّ افْتَتَحَ آلَ عِمْرَانَ، فَقَرَأَهَا، يَقْرَأُ مُتَرَسِّلًا، إِذَا مَرَّ بِآيَةٍ فِيهَا تَسْبِيحٌ
سَبَّحَ، وَإِذَا مَرَّ بِسُؤَالٍ سَأَلَ، وَإِذَا مَرَّ بِتَعَوُّذٍ تَعَوَّذَ، ثُمَّ رَكَعَ، فَجَعَلَ يَقُولُ: سُبْحَانَ رَبِّيَ
الْعَظِيمِ، فَكَانَ رُكُوعُهُ نَحْوًا مِنْ قِيَامِهِ، ثُمَّ قَالَ: سَمِعَ اللهُ لِمَنْ حَمِدَهُ، ثُمَّ قَامَ طَوِيلًا قَرِيبًا
مِمَّا رَكَعَ، ثُمَّ سَجَدَ، فَقَالَ: سُبْحَانَ رَبِّيَ الْأَعْلَى، فَكَانَ سُجُودُهُ قَرِيبًا مِنْ قِيَامِهِ.

رواهُ مُسلم

Hudhayfah ؓ reported that: "I prayed with the Messenger of Allāh ﷺ one night and he started reciting al-Baqarah. I thought that he would bow at the end of one hundred verses, but he proceeded on; I then thought that he would perhaps recite the whole sūrah in a rak'ah, but he proceeded and I thought he would perhaps bow on completing [this surah]. He then started al-Nisā', and recited it; he then started Āl 'Imrān and recited in an unhurried manner. And when he recited the verses which referred to the Glory of Allāh, he glorified [by saying Subḥān Allāh - Glory to my Lord the Great], and when he recited the verses which tell [how the Lord] is to be begged, he ﷺ would then beg [from Him], and when he recited the verses dealing with protection from the Lord, he sought [His] protection and would then bow and say,

'Glory be to my Mighty Lord'; his bowing lasted about the same length of time as his standing [and then on returning to the standing posture after rukū'] he would say, 'Allāh listens to him who praised Him', and he would then stand about the same length of time as he had spent in bowing. He would then prostrate himself and say, 'Glory be to my Lord most High', and his prostration lasted nearly the same length of time as his standing." [77]

Al Nawawi states, "Our companions (i.e. the shāfi'īs), may Allāh have mercy on them, said that it is recommended for every reciter to ask Allāh, to fulfill his needs, to seek refuge in Him, and to glorify Him, whether in prayer or outside of prayer. They also said that when in prayer, it is recommended for the Imām, the *ma'mūm* (one being led in prayer) and the *munfarid* (one praying by himself) to do so as it is a form of *du'ā'* and they are all the same with regards to it, just like the *ta'mīn* (saying *āmīn*) after the *Fātiḥah*."[78] This is the view of most scholars. The Ḥanafis only permit it in recommended prayers for the one praying by himself.

This will not be possible though, unless one understands what they are reciting or listening to. This implies that one's heart must be present in order to attain this *sunnah*.

Ḥadīth no.38

The Ruling of Reciting the Qur'ān Aloud

عَنْ عُقْبَةَ بْنِ عَامِرٍ الْجُهَنِيِّ رَضِيَ اللَّهُ عَنْهُ، قَالَ: قَالَ رَسُولُ اللَّهِ صَلَّى اللَّهُ عَلَيْهِ وَسَلَّمَ:

الْجَاهِرُ بِالْقُرْآنِ، كَالْجَاهِرِ بِالصَّدَقَةِ، وَالْمُسِرُّ بِالْقُرْآنِ، كَالْمُسِرِّ بِالصَّدَقَةِ.

رَوَاهُ التِّرْمِذِي

'Uqbah bin 'Āmir al Juhani narrated that the Messenger of Allah ﷺ said, "The one who recites the Qur'ān aloud is like the one who gives charity publicly, and the one who recites the Qur'ān quietly is like the one who gives charity secretly."[79]

Al Ṭībī stated that there are reports that mention the virtue of both reciting the Qur'ān quietly as well as aloud. Such reports can be combined in the following way:

- Reciting quietly is better for the one who fears ostentation (*riyā'*).
- Whereas reciting aloud is better for the one that does not fear it on condition that they do not harm others by their recitation, e.g. someone who is in prayer or is asleep. This is better, for in reciting aloud one can benefit others by allowing them to listen to the Qur'ān and to learn from their recitation. Moreover, it is a means of openly manifesting one's religion. It also makes the reader more alert and less likely to become tired and drowsy upon recitation. For the one who can manage to recall such intentions, reciting aloud is more suitable.

The believer should always aim to influence others in a positive way. Hence leading others by example is a key process in achieving that. The Prophet ﷺ said, "Whoever leads to good is like the one who does it."[80]

- One should not stop doing a good deed out of fear of ostentation as this is what *Shayṭān* wants. Rather, a person should strive to remove that state and continue doing that good deed.
- Reciting the Qur'ān aloud can also be an excellent means of *da'wah.*

Ḥadīth no.39

Asking for Money Due to the Recitation of the Qur'ān

عَنْ عِمْرَانَ بْنِ حُصَيْنٍ رَضِيَ اللَّهُ عَنْهُ،

أَنَّهُ مَرَّ عَلَى قَارِئٍ يَقْرَأُ، ثُمَّ سَأَلَ فَاسْتَرْجَعَ، ثُمَّ قَالَ: سَمِعْتُ رَسُولَ اللَّهِ صَلَّى اللَّهُ عَلَيْهِ وَسَلَّمَ يَقُولُ: مَنْ قَرَأَ الْقُرْآنَ فَلْيَسْأَلِ اللَّهَ بِهِ، فَإِنَّهُ سَيَجِيءُ أَقْوَامٌ يَقْرَءُونَ الْقُرْآنَ يَسْأَلُونَ بِهِ النَّاسَ.

رَوَاهُ التِّرْمِذِي

'Imrān bin Ḥusain passed by a reciter reciting [who] then began begging. So he ['Imrān] said, "Indeed we belong to Allah and to Him shall we return." Then he said, "I heard the Messenger of Allāh saying, 'Whoever recites the Qur'ān, then let him ask Allāh by it. For, indeed there will come a people who will recite the Qur'ān asking from the people because of it.'"[81]

- The book of Allāh was sent down as a means for people to worship Him and not as a means to make a livelihood. This is conveyed in the Qur'ān with the verse: "*And I do not ask you for it any payment. My payment is only from the Lord of the worlds.*"[82]
- A person can ask Allāh through recitation by calling upon Him when passing verses of mercy or by seeking refuge in Allāh when

passing verses of punishment. A person can also supplicate upon completing a recitation.

- The scholars have deduced from this ḥadīth and others similar to it that taking money for merely reciting the Qur'ān is not permitted.
- However, the scholars differed regarding the exact ruling of earning money by teaching the Qur'ān:
    - One group of scholars was of the view that it is completely forbidden to receive any payment due to this ḥadīth and other similar *aḥadīth*. This was the view of Abū Ḥanīfah رحمه الله, al Zuhri رحمه الله and others.
    - Another group of scholars was of the view that it was deemed acceptable and even advisable in order not to neglect the teaching of the Qur'ān. If people were not allowed to receive anything from teaching and reciting it, they would have to leave teaching the Qur'ān and look for sustenance elsewhere, leading to the neglect of the Qur'ān. This was the view of Al Ḥasan رحمه الله , Ibn Sīrīn رحمه الله and al Sha'bi رحمه الله. However, some specified that one should not stipulate a desired amount.
    - The third view is that it is generally permissible due to the saying of the Prophet ﷺ: "You are most entitled to receive an earning due to the Qur'ān." This was said in the context of reciting the Qur'ān as a form of *ruqyah*, but can be applied to other beneficial actions such as teaching people the Qur'ān. It can also be argued that the charging is for the time and effort the teacher gives and not for the Qur'ān itself.

Ḥadīth no.40

The Obligation of Being Sincere to the Qur'ān

عَنْ تَمِيمِ الدَّارِيِّ رَضِيَ اللَّهُ عَنْهُ أَنَّ النَّبِيَّ صَلَّى اللَّهُ عَلَيْهِ وَسَلَّمَ، قَالَ :

الدِّينُ النَّصِيحَةُ قُلْنَا : لِمَنْ؟ قَالَ : لِلَّهِ وَلِكِتَابِهِ وَلِرَسُولِهِ وَلِأَئِمَّةِ الْمُسْلِمِينَ وَعَامَّتِهِمْ .

رواه مسلم

Tamīm al Dāri ؓ reported that the Prophet ﷺ said, "The religion is naṣīḥah." The companions said, "To whom?" He ﷺ replied, "To Allāh ﷻ, His book, His messenger, the leaders of the Muslims and the laity."[83]

❁ 'Naṣīḥah' is a very comprehensive word which combines the meaning of wishing good for others and purifying something from blemishes and unwanted substances.

❁ Having naṣīḥah for the book of Allāh ﷻ refers to showing a great level of love towards it, venerating it, working towards understanding it, reflecting upon its meanings, striving to act upon it and to have one's manners fashioned by its teachings.

❁ It is obligatory to believe everything that the Qur'ān states. Qāḍi 'Iyāḍ ؒ said, "Know that whoever belittles anything from the Qur'ān or the muṣḥaf or denigrates anything from them, or denies one letter from it or rejects a clear-cut ruling or statement from it, or affirms that which it negates or vice versa, whilst knowing that he is doing that, or doubts anything regarding it, then he is a disbeliever according to the consensus of the Muslims."[84]

❁ Showing naṣīḥah to it also implies not abandoning it. Abandonment of it can occur in a number of different ways, such as by:

   ◉ Not reciting it.

   ◉ Not acting upon it.

- Not having full faith in it.
- Not reflecting upon its meanings.
- Not using it as a means to cure oneself from physical and spiritual ailments etc.
- Not referring to it for judgment.

And Allāh ﷻ knows best.

تَمَّ بِحَمْدِ اللهِ

Completed on the 16th of Ramaḍān 1435 corresponding to the 15th of July, 2014.

May Allāh ﷻ make the Qur'ān the Spring of our hearts and make us from its people.

Āmīn

References

1 Qur'ān 15:9
2 Qur'ān 14:1
3 *Al Tirmidhi*
4 *Ḥilyah al Awliyā'* (300/7) & *al Zuhd* by Imām Aḥmad (244/1)
5 Qur'ān 14:1
6 In particular, ḥadīth numbers 16 and 18.
7 *Al Bukhāri* (5027)
8 Qur'ān 41:33
9 See *Fatḥ al Bāri* (74/9)
10 Qur'ān 4:167
11 *Muslim* (798)
12 *Sharḥ Ṣaḥīḥ Muslim* (84/6)
13 *Al Musnad* of Imām Aḥmad (12292)
14 *Al Bukhāri* (5026)
15 *Muslim* (673)
16 *Al Kāfi* (127/1), Ibn Qudāmah
17 *Muslim* (817)
18 Reported by al Ḥakim in *Al Mustadrak* who said the narration is *ṣaḥīḥ* according to the conditions of Muslim. Sheikh al Albāni considered it *ḥasan* due to corroborative evidence (*Ṣaḥīḥ at-Targhīb wat-Tarhīb* no.1434)
19 Agreed upon.
20 *Al Tirmidhi* (2910)
21 *Ṣaḥīḥ Ibn Ḥibbān* (122). cf. *Silsilah* (713).
22 *Fayḍ al Qadīr* (7/12), al Munāwi
23 *Al Mu'jam al Kabīr* of *al Ṭabarāni* (10450). See *Silsilah* (2019)
24 The *Musnad* of al Imām Aḥmad (6799), *al Tirmidhi* (2914), Abū Dāwūd (1464). Abū Sa'īd Al-Khudri ﷺ narrated that the Messenger of Allāh ﷺ said, "It will be said to the companion of the Qur'ān, when he enters Paradise: 'Recite and rise' and so he will recite and rise for every verse that he knows until he recites the last thing that he knows." *Ibn Mājah*
25 *Al Fawā'id*, Ibn al Qayyim.

26 *Mirqāh al Mafātīḥ* (1469/4)
27 Agreed upon.
28 *Ibn Mājah* (1337). Classified as *ḍa'īf* by al-Albāni
29 *Fatḥ al Bāri* (98/9)
30 *Al Tibyān,* p.63 by al Nawawi
31 *Faḍā'il al Qur'ān*, p.243 by Ibn Kathīr.
32 *Ibn Mājah,* (1339). The version of *al Ṭabarāni* states, "The best person in recitation is the one who when he recites, recites with sadness." (*aḍ-Ḍa'īfah*, 6512)
33 *Abū Dāwūd* (1455)
34 *'Awn al Ma'būd* (230/4)
35 *Al Tirmidhi* (2913) & *Al Musnad* of Imām Aḥmad (1947), declared authentic by al Ḥākim and Aḥmad Shākir.
36 *Mirqāh al Mafātīḥ* (1470/4)
37 Qur'ān 42:52
38 Agreed upon.
39 *Sharḥ Ṣaḥīḥ al Bukhāri* by Ibn Baṭṭāl, (253/10)
40 Abū Nu'aym in *al Ḥilyah* (209/7), *aṣ-Ṣaḥīḥah* (2342).
41 *Al Musnad* of Imām Aḥmad (3712).
42 Ibn Ḥibbān and *Ṣaḥīḥ at-Targhīb wat-Tarhīb* (1422)
43 *Al Tirmidhi* (2926)
44 *Abū Dāwūd* (1398)
45 Qur'ān 73:6
46 *Muslim* (780) & *al Tirmidhi* (2877)
47 *Ibn Ḥibbān* (620)
48 *Tafsīr Ibn Bādīs*, p.35
49 *Lisān al 'Arab* (273/4)
50 *Zād al Masīr* of Ibn al Jawzi, (2,370)
51 *Abū Dawūd* (4843)
52 Agreed upon.
53 *Muslim* (791)
54 *Ibn Mājah* (1350)
55 *Miftāḥ Dār al Sa'ādah*, (222/1)
56 *Mukhtaṣar Qiyām al Layl*, p.151, al Marwazi
57 It has also been interpreted to mean 'madness'.
58 *Abū Dāwūd* (775), Aḥmad and others.
59 Qur'ān 16:98
60 *Badā'i al Tafsīr*, Ibn al Qayyim. (338/3)
61 *Al Jāmi' al Kabīr fī 'ilm al Tajwīd*, Nabīl bin 'Abdul Ḥamīd, (234/1)
62 *al Muwaṭṭa'* of Imām Mālik (219/680). See *Irwā' al Ghalīl* (158/1)
63 Qur'ān 9:28

64 Qur'ān 56:79
65 *Al Mughni* (202/1)
66 *Al Tirmidhi* (131)
67 Ibid.
68 *Al Bukhari*. "Sa'd bin Abī Waqqas ﷺ came to us when he had become blind. I greeted him with Salam and he said, 'Who are you?' So I told him, and he said, 'Welcome, O son of my brother. I have heard that you recite Qur'ān in a beautiful voice. I heard the Messenger of Allah ﷺ say, 'This Qur'an was revealed with sorrow, so when you recite it, then weep. If you cannot weep then pretend to weep, and make your voice melodious in reciting it. Whoever does not make his voice melodious, he is not one of us.''' (*Ibn Mājah, ḍa'īf*)
69 *Kashf al Mushkil*, 367/3, Ibn al Jawzi
70 *Al Bukhāri* (5046)
71 *Muslim* (133)
72 Agreed upon.
73 *Al Muṣannaf* of Ibn Abī Shaybah, (499/2).
74 *Al Majmū'* (518/3)
75 *Abū Dāwūd* (4603)
76 *Al Bukhāri* (5054)
77 *Muslim* (772)
78 *Al Tibyān* (66)
79 *Al Tirmidhi* (2919), *Abū Dāwūd* (1333) and others.
80 *Al Tirmidhi*
81 *Al Tirmidhi* (2917)
82 Qur'ān 26:109
83 *Muslim* (95), *Abu Dāwūd* (4946) and others.
84 *Al Tibyān* by al Nawawi, p.112-111